Question-based Bible Study Guide

The Case for Christ

Good Questions Have
Small Groups Talking

By Josh Hunt

Contents

Case for Christ / Lesson #1 / Introduction
Reopening the Investigation of a Lifetime
Good Questions Have Groups Talking
www.joshhunt.com

OPEN

What is your name and, did you see the movie, Case for Christ? What impressed you about it?

DIG

1. State your name and your favorite "Who dun it?" show—Law and Order, etc.

I always start a group the same way–with what I call a life exposure question. The life exposure question does not have to do with the Bible; it has to do with life. It opens the window of each person's life and lets us peer in.

I often encourage groups to engage in a question and answer style of teaching, rather than a lecture style. Sometimes, people object. Their objections go something like this. "But our group doesn't talk. They don't like talking. They like hearing me talk. They are a listening kind of group and I am a lecturing kind of teacher. We are a match made in heaven. I talk. They listen."

Or, sometimes people will say, "I tried to get my group talking; they just didn't want to open up. It was awkward."

Here is what I have found. If you can get everyone's mouth open in the first part of the hour, it goes a long way toward creating a discussion during the rest of the hour. Sometimes, you get their mouths open and you can't get them shut, but that is a topic for another day. Life-exposure questions get groups talking. — Josh Hunt, Good Questions Have Groups Talking, 2010.

2. Who read the Introduction this week? What got your attention? (I plan to ask this question every week. If you don't get any further than this question, it will probably be a good study. Encourage your people to highlight and underline and be prepared to share one thing each week that struck them from this week's reading.)

My friend Mike Napier taught me a very important lesson on this. He led a group meeting where he asked people to share meaningful verses they had read recently. Immediately one person shot up his hand and shared. Then another. Then another. Pretty soon, there were hands up all over the place. It was electric. Did I mention this was a Baptist group? These weren't Navigators.

I chatted with him later about it. I told him I was really impressed about how everyone shared. He said it was an example of planned spontaneity. Say what?

Planned spontaneity—that is when you plan a meeting to look spontaneous. He had asked a handful of people to be ready to share. He asked them to share as soon as he asked for volunteers. After the third one shares it starts to feel normal. We all start thinking that this is what normal people do. We start our days with the Bible on our lap. We share about what we read. This is what we do around here.

Here is what I suggest you do in your group. Get in the habit of saying, "Can I share with you a verse I read recently that was meaningful?" Privately ask two other people to follow up with a verse they have read. Soon, you will have a culture where it is normal to read the Bible every day. — Josh Hunt, *Obedience*, 2013.

3. What was it that really got Lee Strobel's attention and caused him to dig in and investigate the Christian faith?

Leslie stunned me in the autumn of 1979 by announcing that she had become a Christian. I rolled my eyes and braced for the worst, feeling like the victim of a bait-and-switch scam. I had married one Leslie—the fun Leslie, the carefree Leslie, the risk-taking Leslie—and now I feared she was going to turn into some sort of sexually repressed prude who would trade our upwardly mobile lifestyle for all-night prayer vigils and volunteer work in grimy soup kitchens.

Instead I was pleasantly surprised—even fascinated—by the fundamental changes in her character, her integrity, and her personal confidence. Eventually I wanted to get to the bottom of what was prompting these subtle but significant shifts in my wife's attitudes, so I launched an all-out investigation into the facts surrounding the case for Christianity.

Setting aside my self-interest and prejudices as best I could, I read books, interviewed experts, asked questions, analyzed history, explored archaeology, studied ancient literature, and for the first time in my life picked apart the Bible verse by verse.

I plunged into the case with more vigor than with any story I had ever pursued. I applied the training I had received at Yale Law School as well as my experience

3

as legal affairs editor of the Chicago Tribune. And over time the evidence of the world—of history, of science, of philosophy, of psychology—began to point toward the unthinkable. — Lee Strobel, *The Case for Christ Movie Edition: Solving the Biggest Mystery of All Time* (Grand Rapids, MI: Zondervan, 2017).

4. Why do you think Lee's wife had such a profound impact on him?

IT WAS SUNDAY MORNING AND MY BRAIN WAS POUNDING. I PRIED open one eye wide enough to see raindrops running down the bedroom window. Thunder rumbled in the distance. Ugh! I put the pillow over my head and turned over. A drinking binge the night before had left my mouth as dry as cotton. I debated about whether to get up for some aspirin and water but decided I was too tired. It was better, I figured, to ride out the hangover in bed.

Then I heard the sound of a drawer closing. Someone was in the bathroom. A few moments later, Leslie crept into the bedroom to get her watch from the dresser. I peeked out at her and she realized I was awake.

"How do you feel?" she asked.

I groaned. "Not good," I managed to grunt. "What're you doing?"

"Getting ready for church." There was a pause, and then she asked in a very pleasant voice, "Do you want to come with me?"

I wanted to growl, Do I look like I want to go to church? I feel like an elephant is dancing on my head, it's pouring rain outside, I'm exhausted and irritable, and I don't even believe in God! Just take a wild guess about whether I want to go with you!

But do you know what I said instead? "Yeah, okay," I snapped. "I'll go."

I threw off the covers and stormed into the bathroom to shave and take a quick shower. Then I stomped around the house, slammed some doors, refused Leslie's offer of breakfast, and got dressed. Leslie knew better than to try to engage me in conversation when I was in an ornery mood like that. Basically, she tried to stay out of my way.

"Where the [blank] is the umbrella?" I shouted as I ransacked the closet. When I couldn't find it, I said, "Well, we're just going to have to make a run for it."

I had left the car on the driveway overnight. We ran to it as fast as we could, but we still got drenched. That only made me angrier! Muttering under my breath, I drove down the highway so fast and recklessly that when we hit puddles the car would start to hydroplane. That would elicit more swearing from me.

Before long, Leslie started to cry. At first she fought the tears, but soon they were flowing down her cheeks. "Look, I'm not twisting your arm!" she said. "If you don't want to go to church, don't. Just let me go in peace!"

Now I felt bad. Why had I agreed to go with her in the first place? Why hadn't I stayed in bed and let her attend church by herself? Why was I seething with so much rage and resentment that I was emotionally abusing the very woman I loved the most?

If you had asked me back then what emotions were prompting my behavior that morning, I wouldn't have had a clue. Like most men, I wasn't in touch with that side of my life. All I knew was that the recent changes in my newly converted wife, though positive for her, were feeding the worst side of me. My world was unraveling and I couldn't figure out how to put it back together again! — Lee Strobel and Leslie Strobel, *Surviving a Spiritual Mismatch in Marriage* (Grand Rapids, MI: Zondervan, 2010).

5. **What does this teach us about how we can influence others for Christ?**

In the New Testament church, the gospel always moved on lines of relationship—to Jerusalem, Judea, Samaria, the uttermost parts of the earth—in waves that seemed to move outwardly. Have you ever thrown a rock in a pond and watched the waves move in all directions until they reached every edge of the pond? Well, that was the pattern I saw. The gospel of Jesus Christ began to spread through relationships in ever-growing circles.

If you read through the New Testament, you will see the centrality of relationship. It is nothing profound, but it is just as natural as anything can possibly be. If something is genuine in my life and your life, the natural thing to want to do is to share it with those we know. Isn't that reasonable to assume?

It seemed to me that we were always training people in evangelism to go to Person X out there somewhere. But there is no prior relationship established with Person X. Lifestyle evangelism in the New Testament did not begin with Person X. It worked through relationships that had already been established. — Carolyn T. Ritzman, Claude King, and W. Oscar Thompson, *Concentric Circles of Concern: From Self to Others through Life-Style Evangelism* (Nashville: B&H, 1999).

6. How do you think Leslie's faith made Lee Strobel feel about himself?

The insight is this: the more Leslie opened her life to Christ and pursued a God-honoring way of life, the more her behavior had the effect of unmasking the ugliness, selfishness, and immorality of my own lifestyle.

In other words, the more she sought after purity, integrity, honesty, and forgiveness, the more readily apparent it became to me that my own life and relationships were corroded with cynicism, bitterness, superficiality, and self-centeredness.

Leslie didn't have to confront me, lecture me, or criticize me. In fact, she studiously avoided doing that. But merely living out her Christian life in my presence was like holding up a mirror to me. I was suddenly faced with seeing the blatant contrast between my cynicism and her sincerity, my self-promotion and her God-devotion, my inner ugliness and her inner beauty, my anxiety and her peace, my greed and her generosity, my Lee-driven immorality and her God-centered morality.

For the first time, I was seeing myself as I really was—and I didn't like the picture! I wanted to cling to the illusion that I was a wonderful guy who was doing great. But Leslie's authentic Christian lifestyle exposed the real me by comparison. I was being convicted of sin, and it made me angry because I didn't want to face it.

On the negative side, this tended to create an unfocused kind of antagonism, outrage, and resentment inside of me. I couldn't put my finger on why I was so upset—I just was.

On the positive side, though, God was using this experience to help me recognize the depth of my depravity. In light of Leslie's godly lifestyle, it was increasingly difficult for me to maintain my positive self-image as an independent-thinking, successful, basically good person. In other words, I was beginning to make spiritual progress by recognizing my sinfulness—and that's an essential step toward God. — Lee Strobel and Leslie Strobel, *Surviving a Spiritual Mismatch in Marriage* (Grand Rapids, MI: Zondervan, 2010).

7. **John 17.21 - 23. When did Jesus say the world will know the He was sent from God?**

    These verses are part of Jesus's prayer immediately before his arrest, asking that those who become part of his movement will walk in unity. This unity of oneness will result in the world believing that Jesus was sent by the Father. It is awesome to think that the way we demonstrate God to the world is by our unity with one another. — Mark Priddy and Al Roxburgh, "Series Preface," in *Missional Small Groups: Becoming a Community That Makes a Difference in the World, Allelon Missional Series* (Grand Rapids, MI: Baker Books, 2010), 102–103.

8. **Frances Schaeffer called this "The Final Apologetic." What do you suppose he meant by that?**

    FINAL APOLOGETIC But there is something even more sober. And to understand it we must look at John 17:21, a verse out of the midst of Christ's high priestly prayer. Jesus prays, "That they all may be one; as thou, Father, art in me, and I in thee, that they also may be one in us: that the world may believe that thou hast sent me." In this, his high priestly prayer, Jesus is praying for the oneness of the church, the oneness that should be found specifically among true Christians. Jesus is not praying for a humanistic, romantic oneness among men in general. Verse 9 makes this clear: "I pray not for the world, but for them which thou hast given me; for they are thine." Jesus here makes a very careful distinction between those who have cast themselves upon him in faith and those who still stand in rebellion. Hence, in the twenty-first verse, when he prays for oneness, the "they" he is referring to are the true Christians.

Notice, however, that verse 21 says, "That they all may be one ..." The emphasis, interestingly enough, is exactly the same as in John 13-not on a part of true Christians, but on all Christians-not that those in certain parties in the church should be one, but that all born-again Christians should be one.

Now comes the sobering part. Jesus goes on in this twenty-first verse to say something that always causes me to cringe. If as Christians we do not cringe, it seems to me we are not very sensitive or very honest, because Jesus here gives us the final apologetic. What is the final apologetic? "That they all may be one; as thou, Father, art in me, and I in thee, that they also may be one in us: that the world may believe that thou hast sent me." This is the final apologetic.

In John 13 the point was that, if an individual Christian does not show love toward other true Christians, the world has a right to judge that he is not a Christian. Here Jesus is stating something else which is much more cutting, much more profound: We cannot expect the world to believe that the Father sent the Son, that Jesus' claims are true, and that Christianity is true, unless the world sees some reality of the oneness of true Christians. — *The Mark of the Christian* (IVP Classics) by Francis A. Schaeffer

9. Why is the power of a changed life such a convincing proof of Christianity?

As he sat in the jungle, R.C. thought, When they discover my body beside the footpath one day, who will mourn me? An image of a man came to mind that stirred hope within his heart. R.C. had seen the face of a missionary.

He knew the risk of talking to a Christian. Soon after his encounters with the missionary, R.C. became the first Christian among his people.

He decided to introduce Christ to his village by becoming the best husband, father and neighbor. He looked for people who were seeking truth. He developed relationships and then shared his faith.

R.C. was unlike anyone in the community. Although he had not publicly announced that he was a Christian, many came to that conclusion after hearing him explain the true beliefs of the Christian faith so skillfully. People were even saying they no longer believed Christians were infidels!

The council decided they would force R.C. to recant or be ostracized from the village. R.C. was prepared for this day. They asked, "Are you an infidel Christian?"

R.C. said, "Brothers, no matter what I say, you will not like it. Therefore, I will not answer, but I will continue to live my life as I have lived it for many months. Examine what I say and do each day. And then, you tell me: Am I an infidel, or do I serve the one, true God?"

R.C.'s story is one in progress. Even though R.C. is being ostracized, villagers have seen the difference Christ has made in the first convert. —R.B., PACIFIC RIM / Heavenly Father, STRENGTHEN THESE NEW BELIEVERS IN THE

PACIFIC RIM AS THEY ARE REJECTED BY THEIR ISLAMIC VILLAGES. LET THE TESTIMONIES OF THEIR CHANGED LIVES SPEAK TO OTHERS ABOUT THE POWER OF THE ONE, TRUE GOD. Amen. — Beth Moore, International Mission Board, Voices of the Faithful: Inspiring Stories of Courage from Christians Serving around the World (Nashville: Thomas Nelson, 2010).

10. How can we expect our love for each other (or lack of) to impact the world?

But we cannot expect the world to judge that way because the world cares nothing about doctrine. And that is especially true in the second half of the twentieth century when, on the basis of their epistemology, men no longer believe even in the possibility of absolute truth. And if we are surrounded by a world which no longer believes in the concept of truth, certainly we cannot expect people to have any interest in whether a man's doctrine is correct or not.

But Jesus did give the mark that will arrest the attention of the world, even the attention of the modern man who says he is just a machine. Because every man is made in the image of God and has, therefore, aspirations for love, there is something that can be in every geographical climate-in every point of time-which cannot fail to arrest his attention.

What is it? The love that true Christians show for each other and not just for their own party. *The Mark of the Christian (IVP Classics)* by Francis A. Schaeffer

11. There is an old song—"What the world needs now is love, sweet love." What evidence to do you see of that in our culture?

The television show "Friends" centers on a small group of young adults who share two apartments across the hall from each other. They hang together, laugh together, hurt together, cry together, and support one another in good times and in bad. The community they experience with one another gives meaning to their lives. The message of this show is captured in its theme song, "I'll Be There for You." The song promises that each of the friends will "be there" for each other, and it ends with the responding promise that the other person will "be there for me too."

Christian love has often been called the final apologetic. Christian writer Francis Schaeffer called Christian love "the mark of the Christian." Community not only tells the world that we are different, it also tells the world that we Christians have what they are looking for—not just words or a meeting or a set of beliefs. (We do offer words, meetings, and a set of beliefs, but that's not all we offer.) We offer community with the triune God and with people who will "be there for you!" — Rich Nathan, *Who Is My Enemy?* (Grand Rapids, MI: Zondervan, 2011).

12. How much different are Christians than non-Christians?

Throughout the centuries, the church has often stayed in the places others have fled, caring for the widow, the orphan, the hungry, the sick and suffering, earning a reputation of doing good and standing up for what is right. In our modern day, the church answers the call after natural disasters, digs wells in Africa, and delivers the message of redemption across the globe. Those belonging to Christ should have the best reputation of any people in history. God's glory should be reflected in us, not the world's angst. We all know our reputation may be tarnished, but perhaps not as much as we might think. — *Christians Are Hate-Filled Hypocrites...and Other Lies You've Been Told: A Sociologist Shatters Myths From the Secular and Christian Media* by Bradley R.E. Wright Ph.D.

13. Do you think, on the whole, Christians behave better than non-Christians?

Christians, Jews, and members of other religions all have relatively low rates of cohabitation, around 4%. In contrast, twice as many of the religiously unaffiliated, over 8%, are living together.

Likewise, with divorce, 60% of the never-attendees had been divorced or were separated compared to only 38% of the weekly attendees.

If we focus on the line labeled "Christians (all)" we see that, taken as a whole, Christians are committing adultery about one-third less than the unaffiliated. It appears that the commandment "Thou shalt not commit adultery" is, thankfully, still having an effect on the church.

Evangelicals who regularly attend church display far less sexual misconduct than those who attend less often. Twenty-two percent of Evangelicals who never attend church have committed adultery as compared to 13% of those who attend weekly.

Not only did Protestants commit less crime, but also the Protestants who attended church on a weekly basis did so far less than other Protestants. Figure 6.5 plots these differences, and the weekly attendees had crime levels that were about half as high as the other, less-frequently-attending Protestants. For example, 4% of the weekly attendees had been arrested, compared to 8% of the monthly attendees, 12% of the yearly attendees, and 15% of those who never attend.

Turning to attendance data, we see very large differences. Among Protestants, about 10 to 12% of the monthly, yearly, or rarely attending respondents averaged five drinks or more on the days they drank. In contrast, only 3% of the weekly attendees did.

Turning to attendance measures, when it comes to everyday honesty the results are mixed for Evangelicals. A willingness to lie for a friend decreases considerably with church attendance. While 17% of the Evangelicals who rarely attend church would lie to the police, only 3% of the weekly attendees would do so. — *Christians Are Hate-Filled Hypocrites...and Other Lies You've Been Told: A Sociologist Shatters Myths From the Secular and Christian Media* by Bradley R.E. Wright Ph.D.

14. This is a little beyond the scope of this study, but I'd like for us to touch on it. Changed lives are the ultimate apologetic. But, there is more to changed lives than trying really hard to be good. How would you summarize how God changes our lives?

Life is hard. But, Christian living can be easy. Jesus said it would be true.

It becomes easy as we train ourselves to be godly, as a piano player trains himself to play Amazing Grace. Note by note, chord by chord, day by day, train yourself to be godly.

Eventually, slowly, almost imperceptibly, what seemed impossible becomes a habit. You are grateful without trying to be grateful. You serve without having to remind yourself to serve.

This works best in community. We are profoundly influenced by the people in our lives. We need people wo can set an example for us, and we need to set an example for others.

We worship best in community. There is something about loud congregational singing. Nowhere else in our society do people sing like they do in church. There is something about singing. There is something about worshiping together. We become what we behold.

You got to believe. Believe that God is good. Believe that it is always in our best interest to life the Christian life. Believe that I can do all things through Christ who strengthens me.

We are changed by what we say. Speaking the truth, we will grow.

We are changed by pain. Pain is God's megaphone.

We are changed by the power of the Holy Spirit. You can't do this alone, not even a little bit. Without Him we can do thing. I need Thee, Oh I need Thee. Every hour I need Thee. — Josh Hunt, *How to Live the Christian Life*

15. Leslie's changed life got Lee started thinking about and researching the claims of Christianity. We will spend the next twelve or so weeks talking about this, but, by way of introduction, let's talk about that now. Is our faith a reasonable faith? Why or why not?

Critics attack Christianity as unreasonable. Faith, they say, contradicts reason. You've heard the charges: "Faith is a blind leap in the dark"; "Faith requires one to check his brain at the door"; "Faith has been rendered meaningless in this age of scientific and intellectual enlightenment." Sadly, even some Christians divorce faith from reason. This view is neither biblically accurate nor consistent with historic, orthodox Christianity. The early Church Fathers, the Medieval Scholastics, and the Protestant Reformers believed that faith fits the biblical view of reason. As we consider the reasonableness of faith, let's remember that finite human intellect is not able to fully grasp infinite divine truth. But, the fact that something cannot be fully understood by reason does not mean it's unreasonable. Let's consider four points about the relationship between faith and reason. — Rick Cornish, *5 Minute Apologist: Maximum Truth in Minimum Time* (Colorado Springs, CO: NavPress, 2014).

16. Is our faith provable?

Faith is not foolishness, exemplified by the man who started across thin ice on a pond, saying, "I just believe! I have faith this ice will hold me up." His faith was all wet—or it will be shortly.

Unrealistic faith collapses in college classrooms when challenged. It cringes when hearing about newly discovered "proof" of evolution. It harbors nagging doubts when facing a crisis. But genuine faith is believing on the basis of powerful evidence, not in spite of inadequate evidence. To be valid, Christianity must be logical and real with a "provable" quality to it. And as any courtroom observer knows, proof requires evidence. That evidence exists!

The body of evidence for the truth of Christianity is staggering, and I believe the truth of Christianity can be established to a 99 percent level of certainty. The remaining 1 percent is the step of faith you take when you "confess with your mouth, 'Jesus is Lord,' and believe in your heart that God raised him from the dead" (Rom. 10:9).

I am glad I grappled with doubts during earlier days, for it drove me to burrow out the facts and uncover the evidence. I found an intellectual basis for my faith that satisfies both my heart and my mind. This book was written to provide Christians with reassurance about the validity of their faith while giving them a thumbnail sketch of how to answer those who are examining Christianity. Here, then, is a summary of the evidence that demonstrates the truthfulness of Christianity—beyond reasonable doubt.— Morgan, R. J. (2003*). Evidence and truth: foundations for Christian truth. Biblical Essentials Series* (pp. 6–8). Wheaton, IL: Crossway Books.

17. What are some of the most convincing proofs that you are aware of that support the Christian faith?

At the Constitutional Convention in Philadelphia in 1787, Benjamin Franklin said, "I have lived, Sir, a long time, and the longer I live, the more convincing proofs I see of this truth—that God governs in the affairs of men.... I therefore beg leave to move, that henceforth prayers imploring the assistance of Heaven, and its blessings on our deliberations, be held in this Assembly every morning." — Warren W. Wiersbe, *Pause for Power: A 365-Day Journey through the Scriptures* (Colorado Springs, CO: David C Cook, 2010).

18. To what degree have you doubted? What caused you to doubt? Do you still have doubts?

I will tell you my secret: I have doubts.

I have spent my life studying and thinking and reading and teaching about God. I grew up in the church. I went to a faith-based college and then to a seminary. I walked the straight and narrow. I never sowed any wild oats.

And I have doubts.

I'll tell you more than that. There is a part of me that, after I die, if it all turns out to be true — the angels are singing, death is defeated, the roll is called up yonder and there I am — there is a part of me that will be surprised. What do you know? It's all true after all. I had my doubts.

Is it okay if we ask questions and consider objections and wonder out loud?

Is it okay if we don't pretend that everybody is split up into two camps: those who doubt and those who don't?

Is it possible — maybe even rational — to have faith in the presence of doubt?

Because I have faith too. And I have bet the farm.

And faith — like doubt — grows in unexpected places. A few months ago I received an email requesting a thousand copies of a book I had written. That was an unprecedented request from anyone besides my mother, so I was curious about the story.

It was from a young man named Kirk, a high-functioning corporate type, father of three young daughters with a brilliant future before him, who found out one year ago that he had ALS — Lou Gehrig's disease.

But Kirk was convinced that in the midst of tragedy faith was his only hope. And he decided to use his final months to invite the people he loved deepest to reflect on what mattered most.

The doctors told him he had two to five years to live, but he died in nine months. I write these words on a plane returning home from a dinner that his family sponsored, with hundreds of people, where we saw a videotape of Kirk, in a wheelchair, fighting for breath, speaking of his faith in God as the only force that could sustain him.

Kirk's dad drove me to the airport. He told me of difficulties in his life — how his mother had died when he was four, how now in his seventies he had lost his son. He told me of how he had once been an agnostic, and how he had come to believe.

I do not know why tragedy, which destroys faith in some people, gives birth to it in others. Suffering both raises unanswerable questions and tells us that our only hope must be a hope beyond ourselves.

There is a mystery to faith, as there is to life, that I don't fully understand.

When we take seriously the reality of faith and doubt, the most important word in the phrase is the one in the middle.

Because most people I know are a mix of the two.

And it strikes me as arrogant when people on either side of the God-question write as if any reasonable person would agree with them because, of course, they wouldn't hold an opinion if it wasn't reasonable.

Can I be faithful and still follow truth wherever it leads?

Is it possible that doubt might be one of those unwelcome guests of life that is sometimes, in the right circumstances, good for you?

I want to know. . . . — John Ortberg, *Know Doubt: Embracing Uncertainty in Your Faith* (Grand Rapids, MI: Zondervan, 2014).

19. What books have you read that have helped to strengthen your faith?

Sean McDowell's list:

- *Cold Case Christianity* (J. Warner Wallace)

- *Stealing from God* (Frank Turek)

- *Is God Just a Human Invention?* (McDowell & Morrow)

- *Ethix: Being Bold In A Whatever World* (S. McDowell)

- *Welcome to College* (J. Morrow)

- *Mere Christianity* (C.S. Lewis)

- *The Case for Christ, The Case for Faith, The Case for a Creator, The Case for the Real Jesus* (L. Strobel) *I recommend student versions for ages 11-13.

More Than a Carpenter (J. McDowell) http://seanmcdowell.org/blog/what-are-the-best-apologetics-resources-for-students

20. What surprised you about today's conversation?

21. How can we pray for each other this week?

Case for Christ / Lesson #2 / Chapters 2, 3
Can the Biographies of Jesus Be Trusted
Good Questions Have Groups Talking
www.joshhunt.com

DIG

1. **State your name and, have you ever been an eye witness to a crime?**

   I like to begin nearly every class I teach with an off-the-wall question that gets everyone mentally checked in and allows group members to learn something about each other besides their views on various biblical subjects. Some people think this is a waste of time, but I have found it to be helpful. I am careful, however, not to spend too much time on it. — Josh Hunt, Disciplemaking Teachers, 1996.

2. **Who read the Chapters 1 and 2 this week? What got your attention? (I plan to ask this question every week. If you don't get any further than this question, it will probably be a good study. Encourage your people to highlight and underline and be prepared to share one thing each week that struck them from this week's reading.)**

   My friend Mike Napier taught me a very important lesson on this. He led a group meeting where he asked people to share meaningful verses they had read recently. Immediately one person shot up his hand and shared. Then another. Then another. Pretty soon, there were hands up all over the place. It was electric. Did I mention this was a Baptist group? These weren't Navigators.

I chatted with him later about it. I told him I was really impressed about how everyone shared. He said it was an example of planned spontaneity. Say what?

Planned spontaneity—that is when you plan a meeting to look spontaneous. He had asked a handful of people to be ready to share. He asked them to share as soon as he asked for volunteers. After the third one shares it starts to feel normal. We all start thinking that this is what normal people do. We start our days with the Bible on our lap. We share about what we read. This is what we do around here.

Here is what I suggest you do in your group. Get in the habit of saying, "Can I share with you a verse I read recently that was meaningful?" Privately ask two other people to follow up with a verse they have read. Soon, you will have a culture where it is normal to read the Bible every day. — Josh Hunt, *Obedience*, 2013.

3. **Let's dive right in. How can we be sure that the Bible we hold in our hands—and especially the gospels that are the heart of the story—how can we be sure that they are the story of reliable witnesses, not stories that people made up out of wishful thinking?**

The biblical witnesses were very reliable for many reasons. First, the writers of Scripture were by and large contemporaries of the events. Moses was a witness of the events in Exodus through Deuteronomy (see Exodus 24:4; Deuteronomy 31:24). Joshua was a witness of the happenings reported in his book (Joshua 24:26), as were Samuel (1 Samuel 10:25), Isaiah, Jeremiah, Daniel, Ezra, and Nehemiah after him. The same is true in the New Testament. Matthew was a disciple of Jesus. Mark was a contemporary and associate of the apostle Peter (1 Peter 5:13). Luke was a contemporary who knew the eyewitnesses (Luke 1:1–4). And John was a disciple of Jesus and eyewitness of the events (1 John 1:1–2).

Second, in the case of the New Testament writers, all eight (or nine) of them were either apostles or associated with the apostles as eyewitnesses and/ or contemporaries: Matthew, Mark, Luke, John, Paul, James, Peter, and Jude. These were all men who held the highest standards of ethics and were willing to die for their beliefs, as most of them did.

Third, these writers were credible as indicated by (1) their tendency to doubt whether Jesus rose from the dead (Matthew 28:17; Mark 16:3; Luke 24:11; John 20:24–29); (2) the inclusion of material that reflected badly on themselves (see Matthew 16:23; Mark 14:47); (3) the multiple accounts (Matthew, Mark, Luke, John, Paul, etc.) that establish their words by two or three witnesses as the court required (Deuteronomy 17:6); (4) the divergence in accounts that reveals they were not in collusion (see Matthew 28:5 cf. John 20:12); (5) confirmation of the accounts through hundreds of archaeological finds; and (6) the evidence for early dates for the basic material about Jesus' death and resurrection by A.D. 55–60. Noted historian Colin Hemer confirmed that Luke wrote Acts by A.D. 62.10 But Luke wrote the gospel of Luke, which says the same basic things about Jesus that Matthew and Mark say, before he wrote Acts (say, by A.D. 60). Further, Bible critics admit that Paul wrote 1 Corinthians 15:1–6, which tells of the death and resurrection of Jesus, by about A.D. 55. This was only twenty-two years after Jesus' death, while more than 250 witnesses of his resurrection were still alive (see 15:6). — Ravi Zacharias and Norman L. Geisler, *Who Made God? And Answers to over 100 Other Tough Questions of Faith* (Grand Rapids, MI: Zondervan, 2009).

4. **An interview with Carl Blomberg was this basis of this week's study. What do you recall about Blomberg?**

Craig Blomberg is widely considered to be one of the country's foremost authorities on the biographies of Jesus, which are called the four gospels. He received his doctorate in New Testament from Aberdeen University in Scotland, later serving as a senior research fellow at Tyndale House at Cambridge University in England, where he was part of an elite group of international scholars that produced a series of acclaimed works on Jesus. For the last dozen years he has been a professor of New Testament at the highly respected Denver Seminary.

In addition to The Historical Reliability of the Gospels, Blomberg's books include The Historical Reliability of John's Gospel, Jesus and the Gospels, Interpreting the Parables, Can We Still Believe the Bible?, and commentaries on the Gospel of Matthew and 1 Corinthians. He also helped edit volume six of Gospel Perspectives, which deals at length with the miracles of Jesus, and he coauthored Introduction to Biblical Interpretation and A Handbook of New Testament Exegesis. He contributed chapters on the historicity of the gospels to the award-winning book Jesus Under Fire. His memberships include the Society for the Study of the New Testament, Society of Biblical Literature, and the Institute for Biblical Research. — Lee Strobel, *The Case for Christ Movie Edition: Solving the Biggest Mystery of All Time* (Grand Rapids, MI: Zondervan, 2017).

5. **I'd like to look at the eight tests in Chapter 2. The first one is The Intention Test. Let's look at Luke 1.1 – 4. What do we learn about Luke's intention in writing Luke (and Acts)? Writing a book is a lot of trouble. Why did Luke bother? What was his goal?**

Luke is sometimes regarded as the greatest historian of the New Testament. That doesn't imply that Matthew, Mark, and John are less reliable. It means Luke conforms more to our modern notions of historical research and writing. Luke calls attention to the fact that he researched carefully and wrote things in order (Luke 1:1–4).

Luke's Gospel, along with the rest of the Bible, is divinely inspired by the Holy Spirit, so we might say, "Well, who wouldn't be a good historian with such divine help?" Luke clearly did his part to put his books together. In order to get their divine message, we have to see what Luke the writer wrote. That means that careful reading, study, and scholarship are needed to get the fullness of what God has for us in the various biblical books.

This leads me to make a point about which I feel very strongly. When I was in seminary, I often herd that ministers should never preach above an eighth-grade level of word meaning and language comprehension. It seemed to be taken for granted that laypeople are just not intelligent enough to grasp in-depth biblical teaching. Every bone in my body recoils at this idea. It is not only an insult to laypeople, but it means that the Word of God is being shut up from his people. I often wanted to ask whether God had unwisely revealed at a grade level or two above the arbitrary standard? God wants his people to be taught his Word, and we dare not undermine his intention. — R.C. Sproul, *Before the Face of God: Book 2: A Daily Guide for Living from the Gospel of Luke, electronic ed.* (Grand Rapids: Baker Book House; Ligonier Ministries, 1993).

6. Who are the eyewitnesses he mentions in this passage?

In other words, the authors of the canonical Gospels either claim to have had actual contact with the events themselves, or at least knew people who did and then checked it out. This eyewitness testimony in the canonical Gospel accounts supports their reliability and authority as sources in regard to the events they describe. This is the case because they were not written by men who were disassociated from the events themselves. Rather, the authors of the Gospels either personally participated in them (Matthew and John), or they had first hand knowledge of the events through the testimonies of those who did (Mark and Luke). — B. J. Rudge, "*The Da Vinci Code: Historical Fact or Historical Fiction,*" ed. Robert A. Morey, *Journal of Biblical Apologetics 11* (2008): 53–54.

7. John 20.30 – 31. What was John's goal is writing?

Luke explains his purpose at the beginning of his Gospel (1:1–4), but John saves his statement of intention till the end. In selecting material to be included in the Gospel, his goal has been to have people come to faith or increase in faith (disputed reading) in Jesus as the Messiah, the Son of God, and through this faith to possess eternal life in his name. This statement is true to the constant emphases of the Gospel, but also warns against a literalist interpretation of John as if the main purpose were to report eyewitness testimony. — Raymond E. Brown, *An Introduction to the New Testament* (New York: Doubleday, 1997), 360.

8. The first test was The Intention Test. The second was The Ability Test. In this section, Strobel mentions the telephone game. I whisper something in your ear; you whisper it into your neighbor's ear, and so forth until the original meaning is lost. How do we know this is not what happened with the Bible?

We're sure you remember the child's game of "telephone." That's where one child is given a verbal message to pass to the next child, who passes what he's heard to the next child, and so on. By the time the message gets to the last child in the chain it barely resembles what the first kid was told. To the casual observer, it seems like that same type of distortion could infect documents that have been transmitted from generation to generation over 2,000 years.

Fortunately, the New Testament was not transmitted that way. Since it was not told to one person who told it to another and so on, the problem from the telephone game does not apply. Numerous people independently witnessed New Testament events, many of them committed it to memory, and nine of those eyewitnesses/contemporaries put their observations in writing.

At this point, we need to clear up a common misunderstanding about the New Testament. When we speak of the New Testament documents, we are not talking about one writing, but about 27 writings. The New Testament documents are 27 different documents that were written on 27 different scrolls by nine different writers over a 20- to 50-year period. These individual writings have since been collected into one book we now call the Bible. So the New Testament is not just one source, but a collection of sources. — Norman L. Geisler and Frank Turek, *I Don't Have Enough Faith to Be an Atheist* (Wheaton, IL: Crossway Books, 2004), 224.

9. How many of the original documents—autographs—of Matthew, Mark, Luke, John, Paul and the rest do we have?

There's only one problem: so far, none of the original written documents of the New Testament have been discovered. We have only copies of the original writings, called manuscripts. Will this prevent us from knowing what the originals said?

Not at all. In fact, all significant literature from the ancient world is reconstructed into its original form by comparing the manuscripts that survive. To reconstruct the original, it helps to have a large number of manuscripts that are written not long after the original. More manuscripts and earlier manuscripts usually provide more trustworthy testimony and enable a more accurate reconstruction.

How do the New Testament documents fare in this regard? Extremely well, and far better than anything else from the ancient world. In fact, the New Testament documents have more manuscripts, earlier manuscripts, and more abundantly supported manuscripts than the best ten pieces of classical literature combined. — Norman L. Geisler and Frank Turek, *I Don't Have Enough Faith to Be an Atheist* (Wheaton, IL: Crossway Books, 2004), 224–225.

10. The Third Test is the Character Test. Just as in a court of law we are interested to know the character of the witness, so it is with the Bible. What kind of characters were the writers of the New Testament?

One's basic character—attitudes, inner motives, loyalties, standards—eventually manifests itself in his or her life. Christians produce good fruit in their attitudes and actions. But unbelievers, especially false prophets, will eventually manifest bad fruit.

False teachers can hide their true fruit for a time behind ecclesiastical trappings, evangelical vocabulary, and false fellowship. But how they behave when not around Christians will soon enough reveal their true loyalties and convictions. Unless they exhibit "moral excellence … knowledge … self-control … perseverance … godliness" and so forth (see 2 Peter 1:5–8), we can be sure God has not sent them and they do not belong to Jesus Christ. Another crucial indicator of character that we can look for, as summarized by Christ Himself, is this: "He who speaks from himself seeks his own glory; but Hhe who is seeking the glory of the One who sent Him, He is true, and there is no unrighteousness in Him" (John 7:18).

The teacher who emulates Christ and wants to glorify Him is a genuine servant of the Lord. But the false one, no matter how clever, can't hide for long his corrupt character—and the discerning believer will recognize this. As John Calvin wrote, "Nothing is more difficult to counterfeit than virtue." — John MacArthur, *Daily Readings from the Life of Christ* (Chicago: Moody Publishers, 2008), 193.

11. The fourth test is The Consistency Test. Aren't their tons of contradiction in the Bible? How would you answer such a claim?

Dr. Archer, in the foreword to his Encyclopedia of Bible Difficulties, gives this testimony about the internal consistency of the Bible:

> As I have dealt with one apparent discrepancy after another and have studied the alleged contradictions between the biblical record and the evidence of linguistics, archaeology, or science, my confidence in the trustworthiness of Scripture has been repeatedly verified and strengthened by the discovery that almost every problem in Scripture that has ever been discovered by man, from ancient times until now, has been dealt with in a completely satisfactory manner by the biblical text itself—or else by objective archaeological information. The deductions that may be validly drawn from ancient Egyptian, Sumerian, or Akkadian documents all harmonize with the biblical record; and no properly trained evangelical scholar has anything to fear from the hostile arguments and challenges of humanistic rationalists or detractors of any and every persuasion.

Dr. Archer concludes, "There is a good and sufficient answer in Scripture itself to refute every charge that has ever been leveled against it. But this is only to be expected from the kind of book the Bible asserts itself to be, the inscripturation of the infallible, inerrant Word of the Living God" (Archer, EBD, 12). — Josh McDowell, *Evidence for Christianity* (Nashville, TN: Thomas Nelson Publishers, 2006), 76.

12. Compare John 1.18 with Exodus 24.10. How do you explain this apparent contradiction?

I am constantly meeting men who say that the Bible is full of contradictions. When I ask them to show me one, they reply, "It is full of them." When I press them to point out one, usually they have no more to say. But now and then I meet an infidel who does know enough about his Bible to point out some apparent contradictions. In this chapter we shall consider some of these.

CAN MAN SEE GOD?

One of those most frequently brought forward is the apparent contradiction between John 1:18, where we read, "No man hath seen God at any time," and Exodus 24:10, where we are told that Moses and Aaron, Nadab and Abihu, and seventy of the elders of Israel "saw the God of Israel." (There are also other passages in which men are said to have seen God.)

Now this certainly looks like a flat contradiction, and many besides skeptics have been puzzled by it. Indeed, one of the most devout men I ever knew was so puzzled by it that he left his place of business and came miles in great perturbation of spirit to ask me about it. The solution of this apparently unanswerable difficulty is in reality very simple.

We must remember first of all that two statements which in terms flatly contradict one another may both be absolutely true, for the reason that the terms are not used in the same sense in the two statements.

For example, if any man should ask me if I ever saw the back of my head, I might answer, "No, I never saw the back of my head," and this statement would be strictly true. Or I might answer, "Yes, I have seen the back of my head," and this statement would also be true, though it appears to flatly contradict the other. The back of my head I never have seen, but more than once when looking into a mirror with another mirror back of me I have seen the back of my head. What I should answer depends entirely upon what the man means. If he means one thing I answer no, and that is true. If he means another thing I answer yes, and that is equally true.

But someone may object, "In the latter case you did not really see the back of your head. What you saw was a reflection of the back of your head in the mirror."

But to this I would reply, "Neither do you see the back of anyone's head when you are looking at it. What you see is the reflection of that person's head upon the retina of your eye."

But everyone knows what you mean when you use language in this common sense, everyday way. They know that when you say you saw the back of another man's head you mean you saw a reflection of it upon the retina of your eye, and they know when you say you saw the back of your own head in the glass that you mean you saw the reflection of the back of your head in the glass. In the one case you see the reflection, in the other case you see the reflection of the reflection, and in both cases what you actually see is the thing that was reflected.

Now this case is very much like this illustration. God in His eternal essence is invisible ("unseeable," 1 Timothy 1:17). No man has seen Him, nor can we see Him (1 Timothy 6:16). He is spirit, not form (John 4:23–24). John tells us in the passage before us a profound and wondrous truth: "No man hath seen God at any time.

The only begotten Son which is in the bosom of the Father, he hath declared him." That is, this invisible (unseeable) God is unfolded to us, interpreted to us (the word here translated "declared" is the word from which our word "exegesis" is derived), in the words and in the person of Jesus Himself. So fully is He declared, not only in the words of Jesus but in His person, that Jesus could say, "He that hath seen me hath seen the Father" (John 14:9).

But this essentially invisible God has been pleased in His great grace to manifest Himself again and again in bodily form. Moses and the seventy elders saw such a manifestation of God (or a theophany) when they were in the mount. Isaiah saw such a manifestation in the temple (Isaiah 6:1), and in describing it he properly declared, "I saw the LORD." Job saw such a manifestation and was so humbled by the actual coming face to face with God Himself that he cried, "I abhor myself, and repent in dust and ashes" (Job 42:6). It was God that was manifested in these theophanies, so it was God they saw.

We see then that both of these apparently flatly contradictory statements: "No man hath seen God at any time" and "Moses [and the others] saw God" are perfectly true. — R. A. Torrey, *Difficulties in the Bible: Alleged Errors and Contradictions* (Willow Grove: Woodlawn Electronic Publishing, 1998).

13. Compare Matthew 27.5 with Acts 1.18. How do you explain this apparent contradiction?

The four Gospels have unique perspectives but not actual contradictions.

If all four Gospels were virtually the same, critics would say the writers colluded. The differences in the

Gospels show that the writers did not collude but rather represented four different but equally inspired accounts of the same events.

A partial account in a Gospel is not a faulty account. In Matthew 27:5, for example, we learn that Judas died by hanging himself. In Acts 1:18, we find that Judas burst open in the middle, and all his entrails gushed out. These are both partial accounts. Neither account gives us the full picture. But taken together we can easily reconstruct how Judas died. He hanged himself, and sometime later, the rope loosened, and Judas fell to the rocks below, thereby causing his intestines to gush out.

Many alleged contradictions are solved by following proper hermeneutics, like these:

• Remember that the Bible typically uses nontechnical, everyday language.

• Interpret the Old Testament in light of the New Testament.

• Interpret the difficult verses in light of the clear verses.

• Remember that the Bible does not approve of everything it records (such as the words of Satan).

Pearl of Wisdom: A careful probe into alleged contradictions in the Gospel accounts reveals that they are all explainable in a reasonable way. — Ron Rhodes, *5-Minute Apologetics for Today: 365 Quick Answers to Key Questions* (Eugene, OR: Harvest House, 2010).

14. What is the best overall approach to dealing with supposed contradictions?

Blomberg and I agreed that the best overall approach would be to study each issue individually to see whether there's a rational way to resolve the apparent conflict among the gospels. Certainly there's no shortage of authoritative books that thoroughly examine, sometimes in excruciating detail, how these differences might be reconciled.

"And," said Blomberg, "there are occasions when we may need to hold judgment in abeyance and simply say that since we've made sense out of the vast majority of the texts and determined them to be trustworthy, we can then give them the benefit of the doubt when we're not sure on some of the other details." — Lee Strobel, *The Case for Christ Movie Edition: Solving the Biggest Mystery of All Time* (Grand Rapids, MI: Zondervan, 2017).

15. Test five is The Bias Test. How would you an answer a critic who said that the writers of the New Testament were biased and only wrote what they wished were true?

There is no such thing as historical writing that is not biased. Thus, simply pointing out that the Gospel writers had a definite bias, says nothing about their reliability as historical reporters. If we should disregard every piece of writing that contained a known bias, we would have to throw out, not only all historical documents, but also all other writings, including newspaper accounts, the last letter from your mom, and your electric bill.

The relevant question is not whether the Gospels contain a bias—which they do—but whether they are so biased that we have evidence of their forging the facts to suit their prejudices. Many people assume that this is also the case, but is there good reason to suppose this kind of systematic bias?

It is helpful at this point to take a brief look at the nature of historical writing in the ancient world. In my earlier reference to Julius Caesar, I mentioned that he authored the history of the Gallic Wars. This fact counts for standard procedure in ancient history. The chronicles we have of Egyptian pharaohs, Mesopotamian kings, or whoever, were written by themselves about themselves in order to glorify themselves. According to their accounts, they had only victories, never losses; only successes, never failures. It is lucky for us that we can figure out that if King A beat Pharaoh B, Pharaoh B must have lost, and vice versa, but you would never know it from what Pharaoh B wrote.

In contrast, biblical storytelling is remarkably objective. None of the Bible's heros—Abraham, David, Peter, Paul—are shown without serious flaws. This kind of relative objectivity also carries over into the Gospels' portrayal of Jesus. If the Gospel writers had intended to present nothing more than propaganda for their belief in Jesus, they might have served their case better by leaving out phases of their description of Jesus that turn off the unbelieving reader. The twentieth-century philosopher Bertrand Russell lists what he considers to be defects in Jesus' character as part of his reasons for not being a Christian. He includes Christ's colorful condemnations, His cursing of a fig tree for not bearing fruit out of season, and His drowning the Gedarene pigs among the items that he finds objectionable in the Gospels' portrayal of Jesus. Russell concludes, "I cannot myself feel that either in the matter of wisdom or in the matter of virtue Christ stands quite as high as some other people known to history."

Of course, I do not agree with Russell, and I am loathe to cite him as an authority on biblical interpretation. The important consideration is that Russell expresses his personal reaction to the Gospels themselves. Clearly, a set of writings that can turn off someone from the main character cannot be so biased in His favor as not to be believable. You cannot have it both ways. Thus, by normal historical standards, the bias of the Gospels is not so strong that we cannot trust their factual reports. — Winfried Corduan, *No Doubt About It: The Case for Christianity* (Nashville, TN: Broadman & Holman Publishers, 1997), 194–196.

16. Sixth: The Cover Up Test. What does Strobel mean by The Cover Up Test?

 One of the ways historians can tell whether an author is telling the truth is to test what he says by "the principle of embarrassment" (historical test #7 from page 231). This principle assumes that any details embarrassing to the author are probably true. Why? Because the tendency of most authors is to leave out anything that makes them look bad.

How does the New Testament measure up to the principle of embarrassment? Let's put it this way: If you and your friends were concocting a story that you wanted to pass off as the truth, would you make yourselves look like dim-witted, uncaring, rebuked, doubting cowards? Of course not. But that's exactly what we find in the New Testament. — Norman L. Geisler and Frank Turek, *I Don't Have Enough Faith to Be an Atheist* (Wheaton, IL: Crossway Books, 2004), 275–276.

17. Can you think of stories in the Bible that the writers could have left out so as not to embarrass themselves?

The people who wrote down much of the New Testament are characters (or friends of characters) in the story, and often they depict themselves as complete morons:

- They are dim-witted—numerous times they fail to understand what Jesus is saying (Mark 9:32; Luke 18:34; John 12:16).

- They are uncaring—they fall asleep on Jesus twice when he asks them to pray (Mark 14:32–41). The New Testament writers later believe Jesus is the God-man, yet they admit they twice fell asleep on him in his hour of greatest need! Moreover, they make no effort to give their friend a proper burial, but record that Jesus was buried by Joseph of Arimathea, a member of the Jewish Sanhedrin—the very court that had sentenced Jesus to die.

- They are rebuked—Peter is called "Satan" by Jesus (Mark 8:33), and Paul rebukes Peter for being wrong about a theological issue. Paul writes, " When Peter came to Antioch, I opposed him to his face, because he was clearly in the wrong" (Gal. 2:11). Now keep in mind that Peter is one of the pillars of the early church, and here's Paul including in Scripture that he was wrong!

- They are cowards—all the disciples but one hide when Jesus goes to the cross. Peter even denies him three times after explicitly promising, "I will never disown you" (Matt. 26:33–35). Meanwhile, as the men are hiding for fear of the Jews, the brave women stand by Jesus and are the first to discover the empty tomb.

- They are doubters—despite being taught several times that Jesus would rise from the dead (John 2:18–22; 3:14–18; Matt. 12:39–41; 17:9, 22–23), the disciples are doubtful when they hear of his resurrection. Some are even doubtful after they see him risen (Matt. 28:17)!

Now think about this: If you were a New Testament writer, would you include these embarrassing details if you were making up a story? Would you write that one of your primary leaders was called "Satan" by Jesus, denied the Lord three times, hid during the crucifixion, and was later corrected on a theological issue? Would you depict yourselves as uncaring, bumbling cowards, and the women—whose testimony was not even admissible in court—as the brave ones who stood by Jesus and later discovered the empty tomb? Would you admit that some of you (the eleven remaining disciples) doubted the very Son of God after he had proven himself risen to all of you? Of course not. — Norman L. Geisler and Frank Turek, *I Don't Have Enough Faith to Be an Atheist* (Wheaton, IL: Crossway Books, 2004), 276–277.

18. Seventh test: The Corroboration Test. Can anyone spell corroboration? (Just kidding.) What is meant by The Corroboration Test and how much of the details in the Bible can be corroborated by sources outside the Bible?

When trying to establish the reliability of eyewitnesses in cold case investigations, I use a template that I learned from criminal trials (I've written about this at length in my book). One of the four areas I examine is whether or not an eyewitness account can be verified in some way by outside evidence that corroborates the claims of the witness. Detectives are usually able to locate DNA, fingerprint, or other forensic evidence that validates and affirms the statement offered by a witness (sometimes an additional witness is even used to verify a statement). But what about historic eyewitness accounts that were recorded so long ago that forensic evidence is no longer available? Well, here's where I think archeology can step into the gap to help us substantiate the claims of ancient eyewitnesses.

I've written online about some of the archeological evidence that supports the claims made by Luke in the Book of Acts (I've written more on this in *Cold Case Christianity*), but it's clear from any authority on Biblical archeology that we don't have support for every detail of the gospels. Critics often cite this reality as a challenge for those of us who claim the gospels are accurate. But let's take a minute to compare the state of Biblical archeological support with the state of Mormon archeological support. Both the New Testament and the Book of Mormon make claims about the ancient past that can be verified with archeological discoveries. But while the Biblical narrative has been robustly (although incompletely) confirmed with archeology, the Book of Mormon narrative has not been corroborated by a single archeological discovery. Not a single Mormon city has been discovered. Not a single Mormon artifact. Not a single inscription bearing a name from the Mormon narrative. Christianity does not suffer from such a complete absence of archeological confirmation. http://coldcasechristianity.com/2016/why-doesnt-archeology-corroborate-every-detail-of-the-new-testament-accounts/

19. Last one: The Adverse Witness Test. A good example of this is the resurrection. The message of the resurrection of Christ was preached within two months of the event in the same city where it happened. It was an adverse, hostile environment. How does this help prove that the tomb was empty?

Within two months after the resurrection, the apostles began to preach the gospel message in Jerusalem. If Jesus was still in the tomb, it would have been a simple matter for the Jewish or Roman authorities to recover His body, publicly display it, and destroy the growing Christian movement. Moreover, Matthew 28:11–13 reports that the Jewish authorities bribed the soldiers to tell a false story, in order to account for the empty tomb. Thus we have hostile witnesses (people who would wish to refute the resurrection story) clearly acknowledging that the tomb did not house Jesus.

An interesting historical comment on the factuality of the resurrection comes, indirectly, from hostile witnesses. A critic can inadvertently admit to a fact that does not support his cause when he fails to present his own evidence against it. When this happens, it is a good indication that the fact is genuine. In the case of the resurrection, if the opponents of Christianity could have produced the body of Jesus or any other evidence that He did not rise from the grave, they would have done so. Yet there is not a shred of evidence from the contemporaries of Christ that attempts to disprove the historicity of the resurrection. — Dan Story, *Defending Your Faith* (Grand Rapids, MI: Kregel Publications, 1997), 97.

20. What do you want to remember from these first two chapters?

21. How can we pray for one another this week?

Case for Christ / Lesson #3 / Chapter 3
Were Jesus' Biographies Reliably Preserved?
Good Questions Have Groups Talking
www.joshhunt.com

DIG

1. **State your name and what is one favorite Bible verse?**

2. **Who read the Chapters 3 this week? What got your attention?**

3. **Last week we dealt with the question, "Can we trust the people who write the Bible?" This week, we will deal with a different question: Can we trust that the Bible has been reliably handed down to us? How would you summarize the answer to this question?**

   More Manuscripts—At last count, there are nearly 5,700 handwritten Greek manuscripts of the New Testament. In addition, there are more than 9,000 manuscripts in other languages (e.g., Syriac, Coptic, Latin, Arabic). Some of these nearly 15,000 manuscripts are complete Bibles, others are books or pages, and a few are just fragments. As shown in fig. 9.1 on the next page, there is nothing from the ancient world that even comes close in terms of manuscript support. The next closest work is the Iliad by Homer, with 643 manuscripts. Most other ancient works survive on fewer than a dozen manuscripts, yet few historians question the historicity of the events those works describe. — Norman L. Geisler

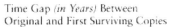

Time Gap (in Years) Between
Original and First Surviving Copies

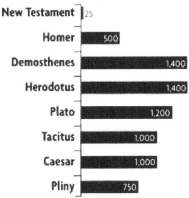

New Testament	25
Homer	500
Demosthenes	1,400
Herodotus	1,400
Plato	1,200
Tacitus	1,000
Caesar	1,000
Pliny	750

Number of
Manuscript Copies

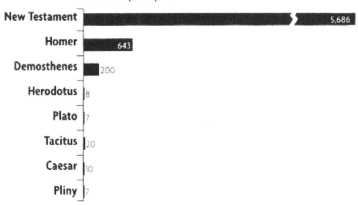

New Testament	5,686
Homer	643
Demosthenes	200
Herodotus	8
Plato	7
Tacitus	20
Caesar	10
Pliny	7

and Frank Turek, *I Don't Have Enough Faith to Be an Atheist* (Wheaton, IL: Crossway Books, 2004), 225.

4. **A related question has to do with the Canon. How did we get the 27 books we know as the New Testament?**

    William Barclay said, "It is the simple truth to say that the New Testament books became canonical because no one could stop them doing so." Bruce Metzger concurs: "The Church did not create the canon, but came to recognize, accept, affirm, and confirm the self-authenticating quality of certain documents that imposed themselves as such upon the Church." This implies that their authority was intrinsic and only needed to be discovered by the early church. Thus, the canon is a list of authoritative books. — J. Ed Komoszewski, M. James Sawyer, and Daniel B. Wallace, *Reinventing Jesus: How Contemporary Skeptics Miss the Real Jesus and Mislead Popular Culture* (Grand Rapids, MI: Kregel Publications, 2006), 124.

5. **There are few places where there are discrepancies between one group of manuscripts and the next. I think one of the best ways to understand this is to look at some actual examples. First, turn to 1 John 1.4 and look it up in several translations, including the King James. Whose joy is John concerned about in this verse?**

    We write this to make **our joy** complete. 1 John 1:4 (NIV2011)

    And we are writing these things so that **our joy** may be complete. 1 John 1:4 (ESV)

    And these things write we unto you, that **your joy** may be full. 1 John 1:4 (KJV)

    These things we write, so that **our joy** may be made complete. 1 John 1:4 (NASB)

We write this to you so **you can be full of joy with us**. 1 John 1:4 (NCV)

We are writing these things so that **our joy** may be complete. 1 John 1:4 (NRSV)

6. **We can't be completely sure whether John was concerned with his own joy or the readers joy. We can't be sure what the Bible says. It might say this; it might say that. Step back a bit. What difference does it make?**

"When all variations are considered, only about one percent involve the meaning of the text. One percent! But even this fact can be overstated. For instance, there is disagreement about whether 1 John 1:4 should be translated, 'Thus we are writing these things so that our joy may be complete' or 'Thus we are writing these things so that your joy may be complete.' While this disagreement does involve the meaning of the passage, it in no way jeopardizes a central doctrine of the Christian faith. This is why the authors of Reinventing Jesus conclude, "The short answer to the question of what theological truths are at stake in these variants is—none." — Josh McDowell and Dave Sterrett, *Coffee House Chronicles Set* (Chicago, IL: Moody Publishers, 2011).

7. **Let's look at two more significant examples. First, John 8.1 – 11. Perhaps you have a study Bible with a note. What does it say about this passage?**

There is considerable doubt that this story is part of John's original Gospel, for it is absent from all of the oldest manuscripts. But there is nothing in it unworthy of sound doctrine. It seems best to view the story as something that probably happened during Jesus' ministry but that was not originally part of what

John wrote in his Gospel. Therefore it should not be considered as part of Scripture and should not be used as the basis for building any point of doctrine unless confirmed in Scripture. — Crossway Bibles, *The ESV Study Bible* (Wheaton, IL: Crossway Bibles, 2008), 2039.

8. How much detail is accessible to the average laymen about these issues?

They are spelled out in the notes of virtually every modern translation. You don't have to have a study Bible. Where there are no notes—which is true of most verses—there is no question as to what is being said. If you want to find our more, there are commentaries available.

9. So, in this case, from what you can tell, should this be in the Bible, or no?

Before beginning our study of this story, I must be frank to admit that it involves us in a serious textual problem. The difficulty, simply put, is that the majority of the earliest manuscripts of John do not contain these verses and, moreover, that some of the best manuscripts are of this number. The best evidence for the story is its presence in Codex Bezae, of the fifth or sixth century, now in the University Library at Cambridge, England. But it is not in the older Codices Sinaiticus or Vaticanus, nor in the Washington or Koridethi manuscripts. In fact, of the older manuscripts, eight omit it entirely, though two manuscripts leave a blank space where it would have come. And not until the medieval manuscripts does it seem to have been included with any regularity. Some early manuscripts attach it at other places, such as at the end of the Gospel or after Luke 21:38.

Does that mean that we should just throw out these verses? Should we place them in the same category as the apocryphal gospels? Interestingly enough, very few scholars (even many of the liberal ones) seem willing to do this, and the fact that a good case can be made out for the other side, should make one cautious in how he deals with it. I am willing to deal with the story as genuine—though perhaps not a part of the original Gospel as John wrote it—for the following reasons:

1. While it is true that most early manuscripts omit this story, it also is true that the story itself is old, regardless of who wrote it or whether or not it was originally in John's Gospel. We find it in The Apostolic Constitutions (third century A.D.). And Eusebius, the church historian, tells us that Papias (who died not long after A.D. 100) knew a story "of a woman who was accused of many sins before the Lord." Later, Jerome unquestioningly included it in the Latin Vulgate.

2. A good case can be made for its inclusion at this particular place in John's Gospel. For one thing, without it the change of thought between the fifty-second verse of chapter seven and the twelfth verse of chapter eight is abrupt and unnatural. We do not know where Jesus is in John 8:12, nor to whom he is speaking. For another thing, the introduction of a story at this point seems to fit the pattern that John has been using in these opening chapters. In each case, from chapter 5 onward, a story is used to set the theme of the teaching that follows. Thus, the miracle of healing the disabled man, which begins chapter 5, becomes the text of the sermon that follows. The feeding of the multitude in chapter 6 leads into the discourse on Christ as the bread of life. The discussion between Jesus and his brothers about going up to the feast in chapter 7 is an introduction to Christ's words at the feast. So, likewise, is the story of his dealing with the adulterous woman an introduction to that speech on the

combination of righteousness and freedom in Christ that the rest of the chapter declares that Christ brings.

3. Third, there is an excellent reason why the story may have been omitted in the early manuscripts. In a contest with paganism, it is easy to see how the story might have been used by enemies of the gospel to suggest that Christ condoned fornication. Indeed, this is the reason for its omission given by both Augustine and Ambrose in the late fourth and early fifth centuries.

4. The fourth and last reason for dealing with the section is the feeling, which many have had, that this story is indeed true to Christ's nature, in accord at every point with his perfect holiness, wisdom, and deep compassion.

As we turn to the story we must see three things primarily: first, the horror of sin; second, the mastery by God of all circumstances; and third, the word of the Savior to the sinner. — James Montgomery Boice, *The Gospel of John: An Expositional Commentary* (Grand Rapids, MI: Baker Books, 2005), 602–603.

10. How much difference would it make to our doctrine if we did not did not have this story?

Out of these 200,000 variants, more than 99 percent are virtually insignificant. Many of these variants simply involve a missing letter in a word, some involve reversing the order of two words (such as "Christ Jesus" instead of "Jesus Christ"), and some involve the absence of one or more insignificant words. In fact, only about 40 of the variants have any real significance—and even then, no doctrine of the Christian faith or any moral commandment is affected by them.

In more than 99 percent of the cases, the original text can be reconstructed to a practical certainty. By practicing the science of textual criticism—comparing all the available manuscripts with each other—we can be practically certain of what the original document said. The sheer volume of manuscripts we possess greatly narrows the margin of doubt. — Ron Rhodes, *5-Minute Apologetics for Today: 365 Quick Answers to Key Questions* (Eugene, OR: Harvest House, 2010).

11. Last one—and this is by far and away the most significant. Mark 16.9ff. What does your Bible (either a study Bible or a note in the Bible itself) say about this passage?

Manuscript evidence indicates that this Gospel probably did not originally include any of verses 9–20. Either Mark ended his Gospel here, he never wrote an intended ending, or his original ending has been lost. The Greek syntax of verse 8 and the fact that all the other Gospels include the announcement to the apostles and subsequent resurrection appearances lead some scholars to conclude that Mark's original ending has been lost. — Ted Cabal et al., *The Apologetics Study Bible: Real Questions, Straight Answers, Stronger Faith* (Nashville, TN: Holman Bible Publishers, 2007), 1504.

12. How old are our oldest manuscripts of the New Testament?

The fragments were found in a cave that had previously been identified as containing material from 50 B.C. to A.D. 50. The scholar who first identified these early fragments as New Testament books was Jose O'Callahan, a noted Spanish paleographer. The New York Times recognized the implications of O'Callahan's theory by admitting that if it is true "it would prove at least one of the Gospels—that of St. Mark—was written only a few years after the death of Jesus."

But even if they are not true New Testament fragments and the John Rylands fragment really is the earliest, the time gap between the original and the first surviving copy is still vastly shorter than anything else from the ancient world. The Iliad has the next shortest gap at about 500 years; most other ancient works are 1,000 years or more from the original. The New Testament gap is about 25 years and maybe less. (This does not mean there were no other manuscripts between the original and the first copy; there most certainly were. It simply means that those manuscripts have decayed, have been destroyed, or are still undiscovered.)

How old are the oldest surviving manuscripts of complete New Testament books? Manuscripts that are complete New Testament books survive from about A.D. 200. How about the oldest manuscripts of the entire New Testament? Most of the New Testament, including all of the Gospels, survives from 250, and a manuscript of the entire New Testament (including a Greek Old Testament) called Codex Vaticanus survives from about 325. Several other complete manuscripts survive from that century. And those manuscripts have spelling and punctuation characteristics that suggest that they are in a family of manuscripts that can be traced back to A.D. 100–150. — Norman L. Geisler and Frank Turek, I Don't Have Enough Faith to Be an Atheist (Wheaton, IL: Crossway Books, 2004), 227.

13. By comparison, how many copies do we have of other writings from this time period?

There are more manuscripts of the Bible than any other single book from the ancient world. More than 25,000 manuscripts of portions of the New Testament exist. Many of these are comparatively early manuscripts; other classical works typically have 1200–1400 years separating the original writing and surviving manuscript copies.

When the surviving manuscripts about other ancient events are ccompared with the surviving Bible manuscripts, it is seen just how good the Bible manuscripts are. Nobody doubts that Julius Caesar invaded Britain, but there are only 10 ancient manuscript copies that confirm this. The earliest copy was made about 800 years after the event. — Mark Water, *Hard Questions about the Bible Made Easy, The Made Easy Series* (Alresford, Hampshire: John Hunt Publishers Ltd, 2000), 38.

14. How reliable are our manuscripts of the New Testament?

Nowhere in the Bible is there a promise of purity of the text of Scripture throughout history, but there is a great deal of evidence that suggests that the Bibles we read are extremely close to the original, inspired manuscripts that the prophets and apostles wrote. This evidence is seen in the accuracy of the copies that we have. Such reliability helps support our claim that the Bible is valuable as a historical account as well as a revelation from God. Since each testament has its own tradition, we must deal with them separately. — Norman L. Geisler and Ronald M. Brooks, *When Skeptics Ask* (Wheaton, IL: Victor Books, 1990), 157.

15. Are the Gnostic gospels on a par with Scripture?

The following is a story from the Gospel of Thomas. Read it and decide for yourself.

But the son of Annas the scribe was standing there with Joseph; and he took a branch of a willow and (with it) dispersed the water which Jesus had

gathered together. When Jesus saw what he had done he was enraged and said to him: "You insolent, godless dunderhead, what harm did the pools and the water do to you? See, now you shall wither like a tree and shall bear neither leaves nor root nor fruit." And immediately that lad withered up completely; and Jesus departed and went into Joseph's house. But the parents of him that was withered took him away, bewailing his youth, and brought him to Joseph and reproached him: "What a child you have, who does such things." [Gospel of Thomas 3:1–3]
— Norman L. Geisler and Ronald M. Brooks, *When Skeptics Ask* (Wheaton, IL: Victor Books, 1990), 157.

16. When scholars see different words in different manuscripts of the Bible, how do they decide which one to go with?

These three facts—many, early, and supported manuscripts—help scholars reconstruct the original New Testament manuscripts rather easily. The process of comparing the many copies and quotations allows an extremely accurate reconstruction of the original even if errors were made during copying. How does this work? Consider the following example. Suppose we have four different manuscripts that have four different errors in the same verse, such as Philippians 4:13 ("I can do all things through Christ who gives me strength."). Here are the hypothetical copies:

1. I can do all t#ings through Christ who gives me strength.

2. I can do all th#ngs through Christ who gives me strength.

3. I can do all thi#gs through Christ who gives me strength.

4. I can do all thin#s through Christ who gives me strength.

Is there any mystery what the original said? None whatsoever. By the process of comparing and cross-checking, the original New Testament can be reconstructed with great accuracy. And the reconstruction of the New Testament is easier than this, because there are far fewer errors in the actual New Testament manuscripts than are represented by this example. — Norman L. Geisler and Frank Turek, *I Don't Have Enough Faith to Be an Atheist* (Wheaton, IL: Crossway Books, 2004), 228–229.

17. 2 Timothy 3.16. What does this verse teach us about the Bible?

The process by which the Bible was written is called inspiration. The term comes from 2 Timothy 3:16, which says, "All Scripture is inspired by God [literally, God-breathed] and profitable for teaching, for reproof, for correction, for training in righteousness." God is the source of all that is said in the Bible. From Moses to John, a prophet is always a man who delivers God's message to men. That message begins with a revelation from God. That revelation might be a voice from a burning bush (Ex. 3:2), a series of visions (Ezek. 1:1; 8:3; Rev. 4:1), an inner voice of the prophet's communion with God ("The word of the Lord came unto me"), or derived from some earlier prophecy (Dan. 9:1–2).

But to be Scripture, the message had to be written too. Second Peter 1:21 gives us a description of this process: "No prophecy was ever made by an act of human will, but men moved by the Holy Spirit spoke from God." That word "moved" means, literally, "to be carried along," like a ship is carried by the wind. God carried each writer along as he wrote so that the message was kept intact.

Inspiration does not mean simply that the writer felt enthusiastic, like Handel composing the Messiah. Nor does it mean that the writings are necessarily inspiring, like an uplifting poem. As a process, it refers to the writers and the writings being controlled by God. As a product, it refers to the writings only, as documents that are God's message.

How does inspiration work? This remains largely a mystery, but we do know that it was done through prophets, as spokesmen for God. We also know that they were not mere secretaries. The secretary model suggests that men were merely taking divine dictation as they wrote the books of the Bible. This assures that God's message comes through, but it does not explain the human elements of the Scriptures, such as style differences, personal experiences related, and different languages used. Neither were they merely witnesses to revelation. Here the human author is seen as an observer of the revelation of God who is making a record of the experience. While his words may not be inspired, the concepts he records are. However, this model tends to neglect the divine aspects of inspiration in favor of emphasizing the human contribution to it, including human error. Such a view does not take seriously what the Bible says about inspiration because it does not include God in the writing process, and it implies that not all Scripture comes from God. The only adequate view incorporates both divine and human factors; it is the prophet model. In this process, the human writer is seen as one who has received a revelation and actively participates in its writing, while God gives the revelation and oversees the writing. Hence, the message is wholly from God, but the humanity of the writer is included to enhance the message. Both the divine and human concur in the same words (1 Cor. 2:13). — Norman

L. Geisler and Ronald M. Brooks, *When Skeptics Ask* (Wheaton, IL: Victor Books, 1990), 144–145.

18. Do you feel confident you can trust your Bible? Any remaining doubts?

SUMMARY AND CONCLUSION

In the last two chapters we saw that we have an accurate copy of the early and eyewitness testimony found in the New Testament documents. Our central question in this chapter involves invention, embellishment, and exaggeration. Namely, did the New Testament writers make up, embellish, or exaggerate elements of the story? Did they play fast and loose with the facts?

No. As we have seen, there are at least ten good reasons to believe that they were honest men who meticulously and faithfully recorded what they saw. The New Testament writers:

1. include numerous embarrassing details about themselves

2. include numerous embarrassing details and difficult sayings of Jesus

3. include the demanding sayings of Jesus

4. carefully distinguish Jesus' words from their own

5. include events about the Resurrection that they would not have invented

6. include at least thirty historically confirmed public figures in their writings

7. include divergent details

8. challenge their readers to check out verifiable facts, even facts about miracles

9. describe miracles like other historical events: with simple, unembellished accounts

10. abandoned their long-held sacred beliefs and practices, adopted new ones, and did not deny their testimony under persecution or threat of death

So we have all these reasons to support the idea that the New Testament writers relentlessly stuck to the truth. And why wouldn't they? What would motivate them to lie, embellish, or exaggerate anyway? What did they possibly have to gain? They only gained persecution and death for testifying as they did. In other words, the New Testament writers had every motive to deny New Testament events, not to invent, embellish, or exaggerate them. Again, it wasn't as if they needed a new religion! When Jesus arrived, most of the New Testament writers were devout Jews who thought that Judaism was the one true religion and they were God's chosen people. Something dramatic must have happened to jolt them out of their dogmatic slumbers and into a new belief system that promised them nothing but earthly trouble. In light of all this, we don't have enough faith to be skeptics concerning the New Testament. — Norman L. Geisler and Frank Turek, *I Don't Have Enough Faith to Be an Atheist* (Wheaton, IL: Crossway Books, 2004), 296–297.

19. What did you learn today that you especially want to remember?

20. How can we support one another in prayer this week?

Case for Christ / Lesson #4 / Chapter 4
Is There Credible Evidence for Jesus Outside His Biographies?
Good Questions Have Groups Talking
www.joshhunt.com

DIG

1. **State your name and one thing you have learned from this study so far.**

2. **Who read Chapter 4 this week? What got your attention?**

3. **The last couple of weeks we talked about the trustworthiness of the Bible. Summarize what we discussed.**

   Although we do not possess the original manuscripts of any of the books of the New Testament, the evidence that it has been transcribed accurately through history is overwhelming. We conclude that the New Testament has been transcribed accurately throughout history. Any contrary conclusion is based either on ignorance of the evidence or on a willful desire not to accept the facts. The late Sir Frederic Kenyon, director of the British Museum, was a respected authority on ancient manuscripts. After a lifetime of studying ancient documents he came to the following conclusions:

   > The text of the Bible is certain; especially is this the case with the New Testament. The number of manuscripts of the New Testament, of early translations from it, and of quotations from it in

the oldest writers of the church, is so large that it is practically certain that the true reading of every doubtful passage is preserved in some one or other of these ancient authorities. This can be said of no other ancient book.

Josh McDowell, *Josh McDowell's Handbook on Apologetics, electronic ed.* (Nashville, TN: Thomas Nelson, 1997).

4. Today we want to talk about the corroborating evidence for the life of Christ. To set the context, how well-known was Jesus during His life?

"He was born in an obscure village, the child of a peasant woman. He worked in a carpentry shop until he was 30, and then for three years he was an itinerant preacher. When the tide of popular opinion turned against him, his friends ran away. He was turned over to his enemies. He was tried and convicted. He was nailed upon a cross between two thieves. When he was dead, he was laid in a borrowed grave.

"He never wrote a book. He never held an office. He never owned a home. He never went to college. He never traveled more than 200 miles from the place where he was born. He never did one of the things that usually accompanies greatness.

"Yet all the armies that ever marched, and all the governments that ever sat, and all the kings that ever reigned, have not affected life upon this earth as powerfully as has that One Solitary Life." — Author unknown / Mark Water, *Hard Questions about Christianity Made Easy, The Made Easy Series* (Alresford, Hampshire: John Hunt Publishing, 2000), 28.

5. Think about this. How does the growth of Jesus' fame differ from most famous people?

On the day after Jesus' death, it looked as if whatever small mark he left on the world would rapidly disappear. Instead, his impact on human history has been unparalleled.

After his disappearance from earth, the days of his unusual influence began. That influence is what this book is about. Rightly seen, this effect on past and current history will cause any thoughtful person — apart from their religious ideas about Christianity—to ask, "Who was this man?"

You can miss him in historical lists for many reasons, perhaps the most obvious being the way he lived his life. Jesus did not loudly and demonstrably defend his movement in the spirit of a rising political or military leader. He did not lay out a case that history would judge his brand of belief superior in all future books. He did not start by telling his disciples, "Here are proofs of my divinity; affirm them and I'll accept you."

Normally when someone dies, their impact on the world immediately begins to recede. As I write this, our world marks the passing of digital innovator Steve Jobs. Someone wrote that ten years ago our world had Bob Hope, Johnny Cash, and Steve Jobs; now we have no Jobs, no Cash, and no Hope. But Jesus inverted this normal human trajectory, as he did so many others. Jesus' impact was greater a hundred years after his death than during his life; it was greater still after five hundred years; after a thousand years his legacy laid the foundation for much of Europe; after two thousand years he has more followers in more places than ever.

If someone's legacy will outlast their life, it usually becomes apparent when they die. On the day when Alexander the Great or Caesar Augustus or Napoleon or Socrates or Mohammed died, their reputations were immense. When Jesus died, his tiny failed movement appeared clearly at an end. If there were a kind of "Most Likely to Posthumously Succeed" award given on the day of death to history's most influential people, Jesus would have come in dead last.

His life and teaching simply drew people to follow him. He made history by starting in a humble place, in a spirit of love and acceptance, and allowing each person space to respond. He deliberately placed himself on a collision course with Rome, where he would have been crushed like a gnat. And he was crushed.

And yet ...

Jesus' vision of life continues to haunt and challenge humanity. His influence has swept over history like the tail of a comet, bringing his inspiration to influence art, science, government, medicine, and education; he has taught humans about dignity, compassion, forgiveness, and hope.

Since the day he did come — as G. K. Chesterton put it— "It has never been quite enough to say that God is in his heaven and all is right with the world; since the rumor is that God had left his heavens to set it right."

Jesus is history's most familiar figure. His impact on the world is immense and non-accidental. — John Ortberg, *Who Is This Man? The Unpredictable Impact of the Inescapable Jesus* (Grand Rapids, MI: Zondervan, 2012).

6. On the world stage, Jesus was not actually all that famous in His day. How famous is Jesus today, compared with other famous people of history?

Yale historian Jaroslav Pelikan wrote, "Regardless of what anyone may personally think or believe about him, Jesus of Nazareth has been the dominant figure in the history of Western Culture for almost twenty centuries. If it were possible, with some sort of super magnet, to pull up out of the history every scrap of metal bearing at least a trace of his name, how much would be left?

We live in a world where Jesus' impact is immense even if his name goes unmentioned. In some ways, our biggest challenge in gauging his influence is that we take for granted the ways in which our world has been shaped by him. G. K. Chesterton said that if you want to gauge the impact of his life, "The next best thing to being really inside Christendom is to be really outside it."

Children would be thought of differently because of Jesus. Historian O. M. Bakke wrote a study called When Children Became People: The Birth of Childhood in Early Christianity, in which he noted that in the ancient world, children usually didn't get named until the eighth day or so. Up until then there was a chance that the infant would be killed or left to die of exposure—particularly if it was deformed or of the unpreferred gender. This custom changed because of a group of people who remembered that they were followers of a man who said, "Let the little children come to me."

Jesus never married. But his treatment of women led to the formation of a community that was so congenial to women that they would join it in record numbers. In fact, the church was disparaged by its opponents for precisely that reason. Jesus' teachings about sexuality would lead to the dissolution of a sexual double standard that was actually encoded in Roman law.

Jesus never wrote a book. Yet his call to love God with all one's mind would lead to a community with such a reverence for learning that when the classical world was destroyed in what are sometimes called the Dark Ages, that little community would preserve what was left of its learning. In time, the movement he started would give rise to libraries and then guilds of learning. Eventually Oxford and Cambridge and Harvard and Yale and virtually the entire Western system of education and scholarship would arise because of his followers. The insistence on universal literacy would grow out of an understanding that this Jesus, who was himself a teacher who highly praised truth, told his followers to enable every person in the world to learn.

He never held an office or led an army. He said that his kingdom was "not from this world." He was on the wrong side of the law at the beginning of his life and at its end. And yet the movement he started would eventually mean the end of emperor worship, be cited in documents like the Magna Carta, begin a tradition of common law and limited government, and undermine the power of the state rather than reinforce it as other religions in the empire had done. It is because of his movement that language such as "We hold these truths to be self-evident, that all men are created equal; that they are endowed by their Creator with certain unalienable rights" entered history.

The Roman Empire into which Jesus was born could be splendid but also cruel, especially for the malformed and diseased and enslaved. This one teacher had said, "Whatever you did for one of the least of these ..., you did for me." An idea slowly emerged that the suffering of every single individual human being matters and that those who are able to help ought to do so. Hospitals and relief efforts of all kinds emerged from this movement; even today they often carry names that remind us of him and his teachings. — John Ortberg, *Who Is This Man? The Unpredictable Impact of the Inescapable Jesus* (Grand Rapids, MI: Zondervan, 2012).

7. **So, let's go back and look at the corroborating evidence for Jesus—that is, the evidence outside of the Bible itself. We start with Josephus. It is not a name that appears in the Bible, but a name that would be helpful for students of the Bible to know. Who was Josephus? (You might do a search of Amazon for his works.)**

   Josephus was a Jewish historian born in AD 37. In The Antiquities (20:9 and 18:3), he corroborates that Jesus was the leader of Christians, that He did wonderful works, and that He was a martyr (by crucifixion) for the Christian cause. — Ron Rhodes, *5-Minute Apologetics for Today: 365 Quick Answers to Key Questions* (Eugene, OR: Harvest House, 2010).

8. **So, let me read you a section from Josephus: "He convened a meeting of the Sanhedrin and brought before them a man named James, the brother of Jesus, who was called the Christ, and certain others. He accused them of having transgressed the law and delivered them up to be stoned." (Lee Strobel, *The Case for Christ Movie Edition: Solving the Biggest Mystery of All Time* (Grand Rapids, MI: Zondervan, 2017)). This doesn't seem to tell us a lot. What does it tell us about Jesus?**

   We have already seen that the Bible was written by men who personally knew Jesus or His apostles and therefore recorded the facts of Christ's life based on first-hand testimony. Moreover, extra-biblical sources, such as Roman historian Cornelius Tacitus and Jewish historian Flavius Josephus, also confirmed Jesus' existence and the movement He began. The evidence for Jesus' historicity is so great hardly any scholar ever questions it. Even Jewish and atheistic critics agree that Jesus Christ really existed. — Dan Story, *Defending Your Faith* (Grand Rapids, MI: Kregel Publications, 1997), 76.

9. **There is a longer section from Josephus. Let me read that: About this time there lived Jesus, a wise man, if indeed one ought to call him a man. For he was one who wrought surprising feats and was a teacher of such people as accept the truth gladly. He won over many Jews and many of the Greeks. He was the Christ. When Pilate, upon hearing him accused by men of the highest standing among us, had condemned him to be crucified, those who had in the first place come to love him did not give up their affection for him. On the third day he appeared to them restored to life, for the prophets of God had prophesied these and countless other marvelous things about him. And the tribe of Christians, so called after him, has still to this day not disappeared." (Lee Strobel, *The Case for Christ Movie Edition: Solving the Biggest Mystery of All Time* (Grand Rapids, MI: Zondervan, 2017)). Does anyone recall what Yamauchi said about this controversial passage?**

"That means early Christian copyists inserted some phrases that a Jewish writer like Josephus would not have written," Yamauchi said.

He pointed to a sentence in the book. "For instance, the first line says, 'About this time there lived Jesus, a wise man.' That phrase is not normally used of Jesus by Christians, so it seems authentic for Josephus. But the next phrase says, 'if indeed one ought to call him a man.' This implies Jesus was more than human, which appears to be an interpolation."

I nodded to let him know I was following him so far.

"It goes on to say, 'For he was one who wrought surprising feats and was a teacher of such people as accept the truth gladly. He won over many Jews and many of the Greeks.' That seems to be quite in accord with the vocabulary Josephus uses elsewhere, and it's generally considered authentic.

"But then there's this unambiguous statement, 'He was the Christ.' That seems to be an interpolation—"

"Because," I interrupted, "Josephus says in his reference to James that Jesus was 'called the Christ.'"

"That's right," said Yamauchi. "It's unlikely Josephus would have flatly said Jesus was the Messiah here, when elsewhere he merely said he was considered to be the Messiah by his followers.

"The next part of the passage—which talks about Jesus' trial and crucifixion and the fact that his followers still loved him—is unexceptional and considered genuine. Then there's this phrase: 'On the third day he appeared to them restored to life.'

"Again, this is a clear declaration of belief in the resurrection, and thus it's unlikely that Josephus wrote it. So these three elements seem to have been interpolations."

"What's the bottom line?" I asked.

"That the passage in Josephus probably was originally written about Jesus, although without those three points I mentioned. But even so, Josephus corroborates important information about Jesus: that he was the martyred leader of the church in Jerusalem and that he was a wise teacher who had established a wide and lasting following, despite the fact that he had been crucified under Pilate at the instigation of some of the Jewish leaders." — Lee Strobel, *The Case for Christ Movie Edition: Solving the Biggest Mystery of All Time* (Grand Rapids, MI: Zondervan, 2017).

10. **These are the only two references to Jesus from Josephus. Why do you suppose Josephus didn't say more about Jesus?**

HE WAS A TEACHER AND miracle worker who spent nearly all of his brief ministry in the tiny and obscure province of Galilee, often preaching to outdoor gatherings. A few listeners took up his invitation to follow him, and a dozen or so became his devoted disciples, but when he was executed by the Romans his followers probably numbered no more than several hundred. — *The Triumph of Christianity: How the Jesus Movement Became the World's Largest Religion* by Rodney Stark

11. **Josephus was a Jewish historian. Tacitus was a Roman historian who lived slightly later. He records how Nero blamed the great fire in Rome on the Christians. Let me read you this quote. How many of the details of the biblical story does this quote from Tacitus corroborate?**

Nero fastened the guilt and inflicted the most exquisite tortures on a class hated for their abominations, called Christians by the populace. Christus, from whom the name had its origin, suffered the extreme penalty during the reign of Tiberius at the hands of one of our procurators, Pontius Pilatus, and a most mischievous superstition, thus checked for the moment, again broke out not only in Judaea, the first source of the evil, but even in Rome. . . . Accordingly, an arrest was first made of all who pleaded guilty: then, upon their information, an immense multitude was convicted, not so much of the crime of firing the city, as of hatred against mankind. — Lee Strobel, *The Case for Christ Movie Edition: Solving the Biggest Mystery of All Time* (Grand Rapids, MI: Zondervan, 2017).

12. Do a search on Amazon for Tacitus. What do we know about him?

Cornelius Tacitus (ca. AD 55–120) was a Roman historian who lived through the reigns of over a half dozen Roman emperors. He has been called the "greatest historian" of ancient Rome, an individual generally acknowledged among scholars for his moral "integrity and essential goodness."

Tacitus is best known for two works—the Annals and the Histories. The former is thought to have included eighteen books and the latter to have included twelve, for a total of thirty. The Annals cover the period from Augustus' death in AD 14 to that of Nero in AD 68, while the Histories begin after Nero's death and proceed to that of Domitian in AD 96.

Tacitus recorded at least one reference to Christ and two to early Christianity, one in each of his major works. The most important one is that found in the Annals, written about AD 115. — Gary R. Habermas, *The Historical Jesus: Ancient Evidence for the Life of Christ* (Joplin, MO: College Press Publishing Company, 1996), 187–188.

13. One more Amazon search. This one for Pliny the Younger. What do we know about him?

A Roman author and administrator who served as the governor of Bithynia in Asia Minor, Pliny the Younger was the nephew and adopted son of a natural historian known as Pliny the Elder. The younger Pliny is best known for his letters, and Bruce refers to him as "one of the world's great letter writers, whose letters ... have attained the status of literary classics."

Ten books of Pliny's correspondence are extant today. The tenth book, written around AD 112, speaks about Christianity in the province of Bithynia and also provides some facts about Jesus. Pliny found that the Christian influence was so strong that the pagan temples had been nearly deserted, pagan festivals severely decreased and the sacrificial animals had few buyers. Because of the inflexibility of the Christians and the emperor's prohibition against political association, governor Pliny took action against the Christians. Yet, because he was unsure how to deal with believers, if there should be any distinctions in treatment or if repentance made any difference, he wrote to Emperor Trajan to explain his approach.

Pliny dealt personally with the Christians who were turned over to him. He interrogated them, inquiring if they were believers. If they answered in the affirmative he asked them two more times, under the threat of death. If they continued firm in their belief, he ordered them to be executed. Sometimes the punishment included torture to obtain desired information, as in the case of two female slaves who were deaconesses in the church. If the person was a Roman citizen, they were sent to the emperor in Rome for trial. If they denied being Christians or had disavowed their faith in the past, they "repeated after me an invocation to the Gods, and offered adoration ... to your [Trajan's] image." Afterwards they "finally cursed Christ." Pliny explained that his purpose in all this was that "multitudes may be reclaimed from error." — Gary R. Habermas, *The Historical Jesus: Ancient Evidence for the Life of Christ* (Joplin, MO: College Press Publishing Company, 1996), 197–198.

14. How does Pliny the Younger corroborate the gospel witness?

Governor of Bithynia in Asia Minor (A.D. 112), Pliny was writing to the emperor Trajan to seek counsel as to how to treat the Christians. He explained that he had been killing men and women, boys and girls. There were so many being put to death that he wondered if he should continue killing anyone who was discovered to be a Christian, or if he should kill only certain ones. He explained that he had made the Christians bow down to the statues of Trajan. Pliny went on to say that he also "made them curse Christ, which a genuine Christian cannot be induced to do." In the same letter he says of the people being tried: "They affirmed, however, that the whole of their guilt, or their error, was, that they were in the habit of meeting on a certain fixed day before it was light, when they sang in alternate verse a hymn to Christ as to a god, and bound themselves to a solemn oath, not to do any wicked deeds, but never to commit any fraud, theft, adultery, never to falsify their word, not to deny a trust when they should be called upon to deliver it up" (Epistles X.9) — Josh McDowell, *Evidence for Christianity* (Nashville, TN: Thomas Nelson Publishers, 2006), 173.

15. Matt 27.45. Is this darkness mentioned anywhere besides the Bible?

Yamauchi reached over to his desk to retrieve a piece of paper. "Let me quote what scholar Paul Maier said about the darkness in a footnote in his 1968 book Pontius Pilate," he said, reading these words:

> This phenomenon, evidently, was visible in Rome, Athens, and other Mediterranean cities. According to Tertullian . . . it was a "cosmic" or "world event." Phlegon, a Greek author from Caria writing a chronology soon after 137 AD, reported that in the fourth year of the 202nd Olympiad (i.e., 33 AD) there was "the greatest eclipse of the sun" and that "it became night in the sixth hour of the day [i.e., noon] so that stars even appeared in the heavens. There was a great earthquake in Bithynia, and many things were overturned in Nicaea."

Yamauchi concluded, "So there is, as Paul Maier points out, non-biblical attestation of the darkness that occurred at the time of Jesus' crucifixion. Apparently, some found the need to try to give it a natural explanation by saying it was an eclipse." — Lee Strobel, *The Case for Christ Movie Edition: Solving the Biggest Mystery of All Time* (Grand Rapids, MI: Zondervan, 2017).

16. We have LOTS of writings about Christ within the first 100 years of when he lived. Let's compare that to others. Do a search for "Oldest writings Buddha." What do you find?

The Gandhāran Buddhist texts are the oldest Buddhist manuscripts yet discovered, dating from about the 1st century CE. https://en.wikipedia.org/wiki/Gandh%C4%81ran_Buddhist_texts

Buddha was born in 563 B.C.

17. Do a search for "Oldest writings Muhammad." What do you find?

The story concerns 1,370-year-old fragments of the world's oldest Quran uncovered by the University of Birmingham in the U.K. earlier this year, which made international news.

Researchers like Huwareib are now claiming there is evidence that the written work was commissioned by Abu Bakr, a companion of the Islamic prophet Muhammad, for Egypt's oldest mosque, the Mosque of Amr ibn al-As in Fustat.

A fragment of a Quran manuscript is seen in the library at the University of Birmingham in Britain July 22, 2015. A British university said on Wednesday that fragments of a Koran manuscript found in its library were from one of the oldest surviving copies of the Islamic text in the world, possibly written by someone who might have known the Islamic prophet Mohammad. Radiocarbon dating indicated that the parchment folios held by the University of Birmingham in central England were at least 1,370 years old, which would make them one of the earliest written forms of the Islamic holy book in existence.

The BBC report noted that academics were able to determine that the Birmingham manuscript is an exact match of other Quran fragments held at the National Library of France, which are known to have been kept at the Mosque of Amr ibn al-As.

There has been some dispute over the exact dating of the Birmingham fragments, however, with some British scholars suggesting that the written work actually predates the founding of Islam by Muhammad.

"This gives more ground to what have been peripheral views of the Quran's genesis, like that Muhammad and his early followers used a text that was already in existence and shaped it to fit their own political and theological agenda, rather than Muhammad receiving a revelation from Heaven," Keith Small of Oxford's Bodleian Library said back in August.

Read more at http://www.christianpost.com/news/quran-muhammad-oldest-islamic-text-egypt-mosque-biggest-discovery-muslim-world-153293/#Ktghd6chCorixpA4.99

18. **One more. Do a search for, "Oldest writings Zoroastrian." What do you find?**

The surviving texts of the Avesta, as they exist today, derive from a single master copy produced by Sasanian Empire-era (224–651 CE) collation and recension. That master copy, now lost, is known as the 'Sassanian archetype'. The oldest surviving manuscript (K1)[n 1] of an Avestan language text is dated 1323 CE.[1] Summaries of the various Avesta texts found in the 9th/10th century texts of Zoroastrian tradition suggest that about three-quarters of the corpus has since been lost.[2] https://en.wikipedia.org/wiki/Avesta

A pre-Sasanian history of the Avesta, if it had one, is in the realm of legend and myth. The oldest surviving versions of these tales are found in the ninth to 11th century texts of Zoroastrian tradition (i.e. in the so-called "Pahlavi books").

Dating is uncertain as there is no scholarship consensus,[3] as on linguistic and socio-cultural evidence, he is dated around 1000 BCE and earlier, but others put him in the 7th and 6th century BCE as a contemporary or near-contemporary of Cyrus the Great and Darius I. https://en.wikipedia.org/wiki/Zoroaster

19. Summary. How would you summarize who non-biblical sources corroborate the storyline of the New Testament?

Just how many non-Christian sources are there that mention Jesus? Including Josephus, there are ten known non-Christian writers who mention Jesus within 150 years of his life. By contrast, over the same 150 years, there are nine non-Christian sources who mention Tiberius Caesar, the Roman emperor at the time of Jesus. So discounting all the Christian sources, Jesus is actually mentioned by one more source than the Roman emperor. If you include the Christian sources, authors mentioning Jesus outnumber those mentioning Tiberius 43 to 10!7

Some of these non-Christian sources—such as Celsus, Tacitus, and the Jewish Talmud—could be considered anti-Christian sources. While these works do not have any eyewitness testimony that contradicts events described in the New Testament documents, they are works written by writers whose tone is decidedly anti-Christian. What can we learn from them and the more neutral non-Christian sources? We learn that they admit certain facts about early Christianity that help us piece together a storyline that is surprisingly congruent with the New Testament. Piecing together all ten non-Christian references, we see that:

1. Jesus lived during time of Tiberius Caesar.

2. He lived a virtuous life.

3. He was a wonder-worker.

4. He had a brother named James.

5. He was acclaimed to be the Messiah.

6. He was crucified under Pontius Pilate.

7. He was crucified on the eve of the Jewish Passover.

8. Darkness and an earthquake occurred when he died.

9. His disciples believed he rose from the dead.

10. His disciples were willing to die for their belief.

11. Christianity spread rapidly as far as Rome.

12. His disciples denied the Roman gods and worshiped Jesus as God.

In light of these non-Christian references, the theory that Jesus never existed is clearly unreasonable. How could non-Christian writers collectively reveal a storyline congruent with the New Testament if Jesus never existed?

But the implications run even deeper than that. What does this say about the New Testament? On the face of it, non-Christian sources affirm the New Testament. While the non-Christian authors don't say they believe in the Resurrection, they report that the disciples certainly believed it. — Norman L. Geisler and Frank Turek, *I Don't Have Enough Faith to Be an Atheist* (Wheaton, IL: Crossway Books, 2004), 222–223.

20. How can we support one another in prayer this week?

Case for Christ / Lesson #5 / Ch.
Does Archaeology Confirm or Con
Jesus' Biographies?
Good Questions Have Groups Talking
www.joshhunt.com

You might show a video like this https://www.youtube.
com/watch?v=e5Fjth9T12U If you are not set up to show it
in your group, you might email your people and ask them
to view this ahead of time.

DIG

1. **State your name and… Have you ever been out in the wilderness and found something really old—an old arrowhead or something?**

2. **Who read Chapter 5 this week? What got your attention?**

3. **This week's interview is with John McRay. What is his expertise? What do you recall about him?**

   When scholars and students study archaeology, many turn to John McRay's thorough and dispassionate 432-page textbook Archaeology and the New Testament. When the Arts and Entertainment Television Network wanted to ensure the accuracy of its "Mysteries of the Bible" program, they called McRay as well. And when National Geographic needed a scientist who could explain the intricacies of the biblical world, again the phone rang in McRay's office at well-respected Wheaton College in suburban Chicago.

Having studied at Hebrew University, the École Biblique et Archéologique Française in Jerusalem, Vanderbilt University Divinity School, and the University of Chicago (where he earned his doctorate in 1967), McRay was a professor of New Testament and archaeology at Wheaton for more than fifteen years. His articles have appeared in seventeen encyclopedias and dictionaries, his research has been featured in the Bulletin of the Near East Archaeology Society and other academic journals, and he has presented twenty-nine scholarly papers at professional societies.

McRay is also a former research associate and trustee of the W. F. Albright Institute of Archaeological Research in Jerusalem; a former trustee of the American Schools of Oriental Research; a trustee of the Near East Archaeological Society; and a member of the editorial boards of Archaeology in the Biblical World and the Bulletin for Biblical Research, which is published by the Institute for Biblical Research. — Lee Strobel, *The Case for Christ Movie Edition: Solving the Biggest Mystery of All Time* (Grand Rapids, MI: Zondervan, 2017).

4. **What can archaeology do for us? How did McRay explain it? What can archaeology not do?**

In trying to determine if a witness is being truthful, journalists and lawyers will test all the elements of his or her testimony that can be tested. If this investigation reveals that the person was wrong in those details, this casts considerable doubt on the veracity of his or her entire story. However, if the minutiae check out, this is some indication—not conclusive proof but some evidence—that maybe the witness is being reliable in his or her overall account.

For instance, if a man were telling about a trip he took from St. Louis to Chicago, and he mentioned that he had stopped in Springfield, Illinois, to see the movie Titanic at the Odeon Theater and that he had eaten a large Clark bar he bought at the concession counter, investigators could determine whether such a theater exists in Springfield as well as if it was showing this particular film and selling this specific brand and size of candy bar at the time he said he was there. If their findings contradict what the person claimed, this seriously tarnishes his trustworthiness. If the details check out, this doesn't prove that his entire story is true, but it does enhance his reputation for being accurate.

In a sense, this is what archaeology accomplishes. The premise is that if an ancient historian's incidental details check out to be accurate time after time, this increases our confidence in other material that the historian wrote but that cannot be as readily cross-checked.

So I asked McRay for his professional opinion. "Does archaeology affirm or undermine the New Testament when it checks out the details in those accounts?"

McRay was quick to answer. "Oh, there's no question that the credibility of the New Testament is enhanced," he said, "just as the credibility of any ancient document is enhanced when you excavate and find that the author was accurate in talking about a particular place or event." — Lee Strobel, *The Case for Christ Movie Edition: Solving the Biggest Mystery of All Time* (Grand Rapids, MI: Zondervan, 2017).

5. What do you recall about Luke's accuracy as a historian?

Sir William Ramsay was one of the greatest archaeologists of modern times, undertaking extensive archaeological work in Asia Minor (modern Turkey). Initially, he started this work as an unbeliever who was thoroughly convinced that the book of Acts was the product of the second century and not written by Luke, a first-century historian. One of his goals was to prove that the history of the first century was inaccurate.

His beliefs were drastically changed when his archaeological finds confirmed the accuracy of the book of Acts in even its minutest detail.

Acts 14:6 "But they found out about it [a Jewish plot against Paul and Barnabas] and fled to the Lycaonian cities of Lystra and Derbe and to the surrounding country." Acts 14:6

In the nineteenth century, Acts 14:6 was consistently presented as an example of a historical error. The verse portrays Paul and Barnabas as entering the province of Lycaonia when they came to Lystra and Derbe. The problem was that Iconium, the city from which they had fled, was also in the province of Lycaonia.

Ramsay checked out this passage in his quest to prove the historical inaccuracy of Acts. His archaeological discoveries showed that Iconium was made a part of Phrygia only during AD 37–72: both before and after this it was part of Lycaonia.

Thus we find that Luke's statement was written in the one and only period of history in which it would be accurate! — Mark Water, *The Bible and Science Made Easy, The Made Easy Series* (Alresford, Hampshire: John Hunt Publishers Ltd, 2001), 30.

6. What would be some examples of Luke's historical accuracy?

Classical scholar and historian Colin Hemer chronicles Luke's accuracy in the book of Acts verse by verse. With painstaking detail, Hemer identifies 84 facts in the last 16 chapters of Acts that have been confirmed by historical and archaeological research. As you read the following list, keep in mind that Luke did not have access to modern-day maps or nautical charts. Luke accurately records:

1. the natural crossing between correctly named ports (Acts 13:4–5)

2. the proper port (Perga) along the direct destination of a ship crossing from Cyprus (13:13)

3. the proper location of Lycaonia (14:6)

4. the unusual but correct declension of the name Lystra (14:6)

5. the correct language spoken in Lystra—Lycaonian (14:11)

6. two gods known to be so associated—Zeus and Hermes (14:12)

7. the proper port, Attalia, which returning travelers would use (14:25)

8. the correct order of approach to Derbe and then Lystra from the Cilician Gates (16:1; cf. 15:41)

9. the proper form of the name Troas (16:8)

10. the place of a conspicuous sailors' landmark, Samothrace (16:11)

11. the proper description of Philippi as a Roman colony (16:12)

12. the right location for the river (Gangites) near Philippi (16:13)

13. the proper association of Thyatira as a center of dyeing (16:14)

14. correct designations for the magistrates of the colony (16:22)

15. the proper locations (Amphipolis and Apollonia) where travelers would spend successive nights on this journey (17:1)

16. the presence of a synagogue in Thessalonica (17:1)

17. the proper term ("politarchs") used of the magistrates there (17:6)

18. the correct implication that sea travel is the most convenient way of reaching Athens, with the favoring east winds of summer sailing (17:14–15)

19. the abundant presence of images in Athens (17:16)

20. the reference to a synagogue in Athens (17:17)

21. the depiction of the Athenian life of philosophical debate in the Agora (17:17)

22. the use of the correct Athenian slang word for Paul (spermologos, 17:18) as well as for the court (Areios pagos, 17:19)

23. the proper characterization of the Athenian character (17:21)

24. an altar to an "unknown god" (17:23)

25. the proper reaction of Greek philosophers, who denied the bodily resurrection (17:32)

26. Areopagites as the correct title for a member of the court (17:34)

27. a Corinthian synagogue (18:4)

28. the correct designation of Gallio as proconsul, resident in Corinth (18:12)

29. the bema (judgment seat), which overlooks Corinth's forum (18:16ff.)

30. the name Tyrannus as attested from Ephesus in first-century inscriptions (19:9)

31. well-known shrines and images of Artemis (19:24)

32. the well-attested "great goddess Artemis" (19:27)

33. that the Ephesian theater was the meeting place of the city (19:29)

34. the correct title grammateus for the chief executive magistrate in Ephesus (19:35)

35. the proper title of honor neokoros, authorized by the Romans (19:35)

36. the correct name to designate the goddess (19:37)

37. the proper term for those holding court (19:38)

38. use of plural anthupatoi, perhaps a remarkable reference to the fact that two men were conjointly exercising the functions of proconsul at this time (19:38)

39. the "regular" assembly, as the precise phrase is attested elsewhere (19:39)

40. use of precise ethnic designation, beroiaios (20:4)

41. employment of the ethnic term Asianos (20:4)

42. the implied recognition of the strategic importance assigned to this city of Troas (20:7ff.)

43. the danger of the coastal trip in this location (20:13)

44. the correct sequence of places (20:14–15)

45. the correct name of the city as a neuter plural (Patara) (21:1)

46. the appropriate route passing across the open sea south of Cyprus favored by persistent northwest winds (21:3)

47. the suitable distance between these cities (21:8)

48. a characteristically Jewish act of piety (21:24)

49. the Jewish law regarding Gentile use of the temple area (21:28) (Archaeological discoveries and quotations from Josephus confirm that Gentiles could be executed for entering the temple area. One inscription reads: "Let no Gentile enter within the balustrade and enclosure surrounding the sanctuary. Whoever is caught will be personally responsible for his consequent death.")

50. the permanent stationing of a Roman cohort (chiliarch) at Antonia to suppress any disturbance at festival times (21:31)

51. the flight of steps used by the guards (21:31, 35)

52. the common way to obtain Roman citizenship at this time (22:28)

53. the tribune being impressed with Roman rather than Tarsian citizenship (22:29)

54. Ananias being high priest at this time (23:2)

55. Felix being governor at this time (23:34)

56. the natural stopping point on the way to Caesarea (23:31)

57. whose jurisdiction Cilicia was in at the time (23:34)

58. the provincial penal procedure of the time (24:1–9)

59. the name Porcius Festus, which agrees precisely with that given by Josephus (24:27)

60. the right of appeal for Roman citizens (25:11)

61. the correct legal formula (25:18)

62. the characteristic form of reference to the emperor at the time (25:26)

63. the best shipping lanes at the time (27:5)

64. the common bonding of Cilicia and Pamphylia (27:4)

65. the principal port to find a ship sailing to Italy (27:5–6)

66. the slow passage to Cnidus, in the face of the typical northwest wind (27:7)

67. the right route to sail, in view of the winds (27:7)

68. the locations of Fair Havens and the neighboring site of Lasea (27:8)

69. Fair Havens as a poorly sheltered roadstead (27:12)

70. a noted tendency of a south wind in these climes to back suddenly to a violent northeaster, the well-known gregale (27:13)

71. the nature of a square-rigged ancient ship, having no option but to be driven before a gale (27:15)

72. the precise place and name of this island (27:16)

73. the appropriate maneuvers for the safety of the ship in its particular plight (27:16)

74. the fourteenth night—a remarkable calculation, based inevitably on a compounding of estimates and probabilities, confirmed in the judgment of experienced Mediterranean navigators (27:27)

75. the proper term of the time for the Adriatic (27:27)

76. the precise term (Bolisantes) for taking soundings, and the correct depth of the water near Malta (27:28)

77. a position that suits the probable line of approach of a ship released to run before an easterly wind (27:39)

78. the severe liability on guards who permitted a prisoner to escape (27:42)

79. the local people and superstitions of the day (28:4–6)

80. the proper title protos tēs nēsou (28:7)

81. Rhegium as a refuge to await a southerly wind to carry them through the strait (28:13)

82. Appii Forum and Tres Tabernae as correctly placed stopping places on the Appian Way (28:15)

83. appropriate means of custody with Roman soldiers (28:16)

84. the conditions of imprisonment, living "at his own expense" (28:30–31)

Is there any doubt that Luke was an eyewitness to these events or at least had access to reliable eyewitness testimony? What more could he have done to prove his authenticity as a historian? — Norman L. Geisler and Frank Turek, *I Don't Have Enough Faith to Be an Atheist* (Wheaton, IL: Crossway Books, 2004), 256–259.

7. John 5.1 – 15. What has archaeology discovered about this pool? You may have a study Bible with a note.

Over and over again, archaeologists have made discoveries that confirm completely irrelevant, "picky little" details in Gospel stories. If one is writing a legend, one does not take pains to get small details accurate, especially if they have nothing to do with the reason for writing the account in the first place. Such confirmation shows that the Gospel writers were trying to get it right, even down to the level of insignificant details. Here are two examples of this selected from a much larger pool of candidates.

In John 5:1–15, Jesus is supposed to have healed a man at a place called the pool of Bethesda. The passage says that the pool was surrounded by five porticos (rows of columns supporting a roof). Until the 1890s, critics dismissed the entire narrative on the grounds that no one had ever discovered the pool. But, then, archaeologists discovered the pool, and it had exactly five porticoes, just as John said. — J. P. Moreland, *Love Your God with All Your Mind: The Role of Reason in the Life of the Soul* (Colorado Springs, CO: NavPress, 2012), 211–212.

8. **Luke 2 contains the story of the census that was to be take of the entire Roman world. Yet, some say no record of a census has been found. Your response?**

The Worldwide Census. Luke 2:1–3 refers to a worldwide census under Caesar Augustus when Quirinius was governor of Syria. However, according to the annals of ancient history, no such census took place. In fact, Quirinius did not become governor in Syria until A.D. 6. It was commonly held by critics that Luke erred in his assertion about a registration under Caesar Augustus, and that the census actually took place in A.D. 6 or 7 (which is mentioned by Luke in Gamaliel's speech recorded in Acts 5:37).

A Possible Retranslation. F. F. Bruce offers another possibility. The Greek of Luke 2:2 can be translated: "This enrollment (census) was before that made when Quirinius was governor of Syria." In this case, the Greek word translated "first" (prōtos) is translated as a comparative, "before." Because of the construction of the sentence, this is not an unlikely reading. In this case there is no problem, since that census of A.D. 6 is well known to historians.

Recent Archaeological Support. The lack of any extrabiblical support led some to claim this an error. However, with recent scholarship, it is now widely admitted that there was in fact an earlier registration, as Luke records.

William Ramsay discovered several inscriptions that indicated that Quirinius was governor of Syria on two occasions, the first time several years prior to A.D. 6. According to the very papers that recorded the censuses, (see Ramsay, Was Christ?) there was in fact a census between 10 and 5 B.C. Periodic registrations took place every fourteen years. Because of this regular pattern of census taking, any such action was regarded as the general policy of Augustus, even though a local census may have been instigated by a local governor. Therefore, Luke recognizes the census as stemming from the decree of Augustus. — Norman L. Geisler, "Luke, Alleged Errors In," *Baker Encyclopedia of Christian Apologetics, Baker Reference Library* (Grand Rapids, MI: Baker Books, 1999), 430–431.

9. Matthew 2.23 records that Joseph took his family to Nazareth. Some say no record of Nazareth has ever been found. You say?

Did Nazareth exist during the life of Jesus? How can we know? What does the evidence say? These are questions to which Christians have been asked to give an answer on a more and more frequent basis by those who profess themselves to be "skeptics" in our world today. It is curious that the first-century historicity of Jesus should be the subject of such contention, since this matter was effectively laid to rest long ago.

There are several reasons which are often given for doubting the first-century historicity of Nazareth, which are largely built around arguments from silence. For one thing, Nazareth is never mentioned in the writings of Josephus, nor is it mentioned in any other first-century writings. Critics also contend that the biblical geography is in error, as there is no cliff near the synagogue from which Jesus was allegedly thrown, as recounted in Luke 4:24–30.

Generally speaking, caution should be taken when dealing with arguments from silence. The question must be raised as to just how much one would expect the contemporary writers to mention the town of Nazareth. Nazareth was a small and insignificant village, and Josephus had no real reason to mention it. The town's insignificance is evident in the first chapter of John's gospel, when Nathaniel asks, "Nazareth! Can anything good come from there?" (John 1:46).

Leaving aside the problems with the argument from silence, it should also be noted that the claim is not entirely correct. In AD 70, at the end of the Jewish war with the Romans, the temple in Jerusalem was destroyed, and this meant that Jewish priests and their families had to be redeployed. An inscription was discovered in 1962 in Caesarea Maritima, which documented that the priests of the order of Elkalir came to live in Nazareth. This has only been confirmed by later discoveries. For example, in 2009, the first Nazarene home to date from Jesus' era was excavated by archaeologists. The house was a simple structure, consisting of two small rooms and a courtyard.

The claim about the errant geography carries a bit more weight than the argument from silence. The closest cliff from which Jesus might have been thrown is roughly 2.5 miles away from the synagogue, however, and there is no reason why Jesus could not have been taken this far.

In conclusion, the claim that there is no historical evidence for the existence of the town of Nazareth in the first century stands refuted by the archaeological data, and many of the more informed atheist critics, even among those who deny the historicity of Jesus, have advised caution with this argument. — Got Questions Ministries, *Got Questions? Bible Questions*

Answered (Bellingham, WA: Logos Bible Software, 2002–2013).

10. Matthew 2.13ff recounts the slaughter of babies around the time of Jesus' birth. Surely this horrific event would have been recorded elsewhere. How do we explain the silence on this?

WE have already seen that Herod was a past master in the art of assassination. He had no sooner come to the throne than he began by annihilating the Sanhedrin, the supreme court of the Jews. Later he slaughtered 300 court officers out of hand. Later still he murdered his wife Mariamne, and her mother Alexandra, his eldest son Antipater, and two other sons, Alexander and Aristobulus. And in the hour of his death he arranged for the slaughter of the notable men of Jerusalem.

It was not to be expected that Herod would calmly accept the news that a child had been born who was going to be king. We have read how he had carefully inquired of the wise men when they had seen the star. Even then, he was craftily working out the age of the child so that he might take steps towards murder; and now he put his plans into swift and savage action. He gave orders that every child under two years of age in Bethlehem and the surrounding district should be slaughtered.

There are two things which we must note. First, Bethlehem was not a large town, and the number of the children would not be greater than twenty to thirty babies. We must not think in terms of hundreds. It is true that this does not make Herod's crime any the less terrible, but we must get the picture right.

Second, there are certain critics who hold that this slaughter cannot have taken place because there is no mention of it in any writer outside this one passage of the New Testament. The Jewish historian Josephus, for instance, does not mention it. There are two things to be said. First, as we have just seen, Bethlehem was a comparatively small place, and in a land where murder was so widespread the slaughter of twenty or thirty babies would cause little stir, and would mean very little except to the broken-hearted mothers of Bethlehem. Second, the nineteenth-century historian Thomas Macaulay, in his famous History of England, points out that John Evelyn, the well-known seventeenth-century diarist, who was a most assiduous and voluminous recorder of contemporary events, never mentions the massacre of Glencoe. The fact that a thing is not mentioned, even in the places where one might expect it to be mentioned, is no proof at all that it did not happen. The whole incident is so typical of Herod that we need not doubt that Matthew is passing the truth down to us. — William Barclay, *The Gospel of Matthew, Third Ed., The New Daily Study Bible* (Edinburgh: Saint Andrew Press, 2001), 42–43.

11. What do we know about this Herod that slaughtered these babies?

Herod ruled in a time when only the ruthless survived. He cowered before no one. He had ten or eleven wives. He suspected the ambitions of the only one he ever truly loved, so he had her executed. He also had his mother-in-law, two of his brothers-in-law, and two of his own sons by his favorite wife executed. When his old barber tried to stick up for his sons, he had his barber executed. Caesar remarked that (given the Jewish refusal to eat pork) it was better to be Herod's pig than his son. Herod rewarded his friends and punished his enemies, the sign of a great-souled man in his day.

Jesus, when he was a man, would be nearly as silent and passive before Herod's successor as he was when he was a baby before Herod.

Herod clung to his title to the end. While he was dying, he had a group of protestors arrested, the ringleaders burned alive, and the rest executed. Five days before his death, he had another son executed for trying to grab power prematurely. His will instructed scores of prominent Israelites be executed on the day he died so there would be weeping in Israel. — John Ortberg, *Who Is This Man? The Unpredictable Impact of the Inescapable Jesus* (Grand Rapids, MI: Zondervan, 2012).

12. Do a search on your smart phone for pictures of the Dead Sea Scrolls, or where they were found.

13. What is the story of this famous discovery?

Ralph Earle gives a vivid and concise answer to how the scrolls were found, by sharing an account showing God's providential care:

The story of this discovery is one of the most fascinating tales of modern times. In February or March of 1947 a Bedouin shepherd boy named Muhammad was searching for a lost goat. He tossed a stone into a hole in a cliff on the west side of the Dead Sea, about eight miles south of Jericho. To his surprise he heard the sound of shattering pottery. Investigating, he discovered an amazing sight. On the floor of the cave were several large jars containing leather scrolls, wrapped in linen cloth. Because the jars were carefully sealed, the scrolls had been preserved in excellent condition for nearly 1,900 years. (They were evidently placed there in A.D. 68.)

Five of the scrolls found in Dead Sea Cave I, as it is now called, were bought by the archbishop of the Syrian Orthodox Monastery at Jerusalem. Meanwhile, three other scrolls were purchased by Professor Sukenik of the Hebrew University there.

When the scrolls were first discovered, no publicity was given to them. In November of 1947, two days after Professor Sukenik purchased three scrolls and two jars from the cave, he wrote in his diary: "It may be that this is one of the greatest finds ever made in Palestine, a find we never so much as hoped for." But these significant words were not published at the time.

Fortunately, in February of 1948, the archbishop, who could not read Hebrew, phoned the American School of Oriental Research in Jerusalem and told about the scrolls. By good providence, the acting director of the school at the moment was a young scholar named John Trever, who was

also an excellent amateur photographer. With arduous, dedicated labor he photographed each column of the great Isaiah scroll, which is 24 feet long and 10 inches high. He developed the plates himself and sent a few prints by airmail to Dr. W. F. Albright of Johns Hopkins University, who was widely recognized as the dean of American biblical archaeologists. By return airmail Albright wrote: "My heartiest congratulations on the greatest manuscript discovery of modern times!...What an absolutely incredible find! And there can happily not be the slightest doubt in the world about the genuineness of the manuscript." He dated it about 100 B.C. (Earle, HWGB, 48–49) — Josh McDowell, *Evidence for Christianity* (Nashville, TN: Thomas Nelson Publishers, 2006), 114–115.

14. What is the significance of this discovery?

If you had asked any biblical scholar, before the discovery of the Dead Sea Scrolls, what would constitute his dream for a discovery that would greatly verify the reliability of the Old Testament, he would have said, "Older witnesses to the original Old Testament manuscripts." The big question was asked first by Sir Frederic Kenyon: "Does this Hebrew text, which we call Masoretic, and which we have shown to descend from a text drawn up about A.D. 100, faithfully represent the Hebrew text as originally written by the authors of the Old Testament books?" (Kenyon, OBAM, 47).

Before the discovery of the Dead Sea Scrolls, the question was "How accurate are the copies we have today, compared to the copies of the first century and earlier?" The earliest complete copy of the Old Testament dates from the tenth century. Thus the big question: "Because the text has been copied over many times, can we trust it?" The Dead Sea Scrolls provide an astounding answer.

1D. What Are the Dead Sea Scrolls?

The scrolls are made up of some forty thousand inscribed fragments. From these fragments, more than five hundred books have been reconstructed. Many extrabiblical books and fragments were discovered that shed light on the second century B.C. to first century A.D. religious community of Qumran on the shores of the Dead Sea. Such writings as the "Zadokite documents," a "Rule of the Community," and the "Manual of Discipline" help us to understand the purpose of daily Qumran life. In the various caves are some helpful commentaries on the Scriptures. But the most important documents of the Dead Sea Scrolls are copies of the Old Testament text dating from more than a century before the birth of Christ. — Josh McDowell, *Evidence for Christianity* (Nashville, TN: Thomas Nelson Publishers, 2006), 113–114.

15. When we looked at the documentary evidence for the New Testament, we compared it with the documentary evidence for other books in that time period. Do you recall what we found?

There are more manuscripts of the Bible than any other single book from the ancient world. More than 25,000 manuscripts of portions of the New Testament exist. Many of these are comparatively early manuscripts; other classical works typically have 1200–1400 years separating the original writing and surviving manuscript copies.

When the surviving manuscripts about other ancient events are compared with the surviving Bible manuscripts, it is seen just how good the

Bible manuscripts are. Nobody doubts that Julius Caesar invaded Britain, but there are only 10 ancient manuscript copies that confirm this. The earliest copy was made about 800 years after the event. — Mark Water, *Hard Questions about the Bible Made Easy, The Made Easy Series* (Alresford, Hampshire: John Hunt Publishers Ltd, 2000), 38.

16. Let's compare the archaeological accuracy of the Bible compared with the book of Mormon. Do you recall what Strobel had to say about that?

AS WE'VE SEEN IN THE PREVIOUS TWO READINGS, ARCHAEOLOGY'S repeated affirmations of the biblical account—both the Old Testament and New Testament—provide important corroboration for its reliability.

John McRay, who was a professor of archaeology and is the author of Archaeology and the New Testament, said there's no question that archaeological findings have enhanced the New Testament's credibility. And he assured me, "Archaeology has not produced anything that is unequivocally a contradiction to the Bible."

This, however, is in stark contrast to how archaeology has proved to be devastating for Mormonism. Although Joseph Smith, the founder of the Mormon Church, claimed that his Book of Mormon is "the most correct of any book upon the earth," archaeology has repeatedly failed to substantiate its claims about events that supposedly occurred long ago in the Americas, including Jesus' alleged appearances there.

In fact, I wrote to the Smithsonian Institute to inquire whether there is any evidence supporting the claims of Mormonism, only to be told that they see "no direct connection between the archaeology of the New World and the subject matter of the book."

Authors John Ankerberg and John Weldon concluded, "No Book of Mormon cities have ever been located, no Book of Mormon person, place, nation, or name has ever been found, no Book of Mormon artifacts, no Book of Mormon scriptures, no Book of Mormon inscriptions, . . . nothing which demonstrates the Book of Mormon is anything other than myth or invention has ever been found."

Said Bill McKeever and Eric Johnson in their book Mormonism 101: "Many biblical archaeological discoveries are made every year; if not for the lack of funding and laborers, there is so much more waiting to be discovered. . . . When the Book of Mormon is considered, however, there is nothing that can be positively identified to support the names, places, and events written by ancient Americans. . . . Until Book of Mormon evidence moves beyond the realm of faith, it can be rightly classified as a myth, legend, or story without any basis in historical fact."

I understand that there are many sincere Mormons for whom this information is hard to hear. They need to consider it, though, because so much of what the Mormon church teaches contradicts Scripture and the teachings of Christ. — Lee Strobel and Mark Mittelberg, *Moments of Truth* (Grand Rapids, MI: Zondervan, 2016).

17. By the way, besides archaeological troubles, what other problems are there with Mormon beliefs?

We can better appreciate this heritage when we compare the OT to other religious books such as the Qur'an and The Book of Mormon. First, let me give a brief summary concerning general contrasts between these works. The Bible (both Old and New Testaments) was written by approximately forty different authors over a period of over 1,000 years, and yet there is a consistent and clear message throughout the book; neither the Qur'an nor The Book of Mormon has such a pedigree. There is extensive manuscript evidence for the Bible, including at least 300 Hebrew manuscripts and 5,800 Greek manuscripts, as well as more than 20,000 ancient manuscripts of the Old and New Testaments written in various languages, and more than 30,000 scriptural quotations in the early church fathers which help confirm the accuracy of Scriptures. Neither the Qur'an nor The Book of Mormon can make this claim. The OT contains specific prophecies that claim to be fulfilled in the NT (e.g., Isa 53:3–4 = Matt 8:17; Isa 53:7–8 = Acts 8:32–35; Isa 53:12 = Luke 22:37; Mic 5:2 = Matt 2:6; Joel 2:28–32 = Acts 2:16–21); neither the Qur'an nor The Book of Mormon contain anything like this. It is interesting that both the Qur'an and The Book of Mormon claim to be a continuation of divine revelation from the Bible through their specific prophets, and yet both works contain significant contradictions with the theology of the Bible. The book of Hebrews (1:1–2) claims that Jesus is the final revelation, implying there will be no further divine revelation. Now, let's look more closely at the text critical issues of the Qur'an and The Book of Mormon. — Steven B. Cowan and Terry L. Wilder, *In Defense of the Bible* (Nashville: B&H, 2013).

18. Let's watch a video together. What archaeological discovery impresses you the most and why? https://www.youtube.com/watch?v=Wo7CKYPFxDw

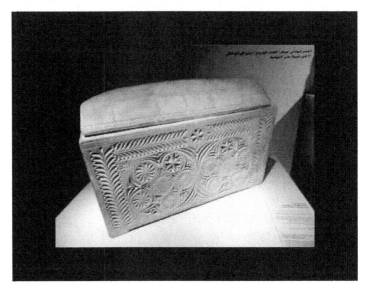

19. What impressed you from this week's study?

20. How can we pray for each other this week?

Case for Christ / Lesson #6 / Chapter 6
Is the Jesus of History the Same as the Jesus of Faith?
Good Questions Have Groups Talking
www.joshhunt.com

Email your people and ask them to do some Googling and reading about The Jesus Seminar.

DIG

1. **State your name and one thing you are grateful for this week?**

2. **Who read Chapter 6 this week? What got your attention?**

3. **This week's interview is with Gregory A. Boyd. What is his expertise? What do you recall about him?**

   Boyd first clashed with the Jesus Seminar in 1996, when he wrote a devastating critique of liberal perspectives of Jesus, called Cynic Sage or Son of God? Recovering the Real Jesus in an Age of Revisionist Replies. The heavily footnoted, 416-page tome was honored by readers of Christianity Today as one of their favorite books of the year. His popular paperback Jesus under Siege continues the same themes on a more introductory level.

   Boyd's other books include the award-winning Letters from a Skeptic, in which he and his then-doubting father wrestle through tough issues involving Christianity (culminating in his father becoming a committed

Christian), and God at War: The Bible and Spiritual Conflict. He also co-authored The Jesus Legend: A Case for the Historical Reliability of the Synoptic Jesus Tradition. In addition, he was a contributing scholar to The Quest Study Bible, which was designed for people who are asking intellectual questions about the Christian faith. — Lee Strobel, *The Case for Christ Movie Edition: Solving the Biggest Mystery of All Time* (Grand Rapids, MI: Zondervan, 2017).

4. Strobel spilled a lot of ink this week talking about the Jesus Seminar. What is the Jesus Seminar?

The Jesus Seminar is a controversial research team of academic New Testament scholars founded in 1985 by the late Robert Funk under the auspices of the Westar Institute. It is a relatively new corporate venture that attempts, by a process of discussion and voting, to arrive at an answer to two questions: "What did Jesus really say?" and "What did Jesus really do?" It is a continuation of the "quest for the Historical Jesus" movement of the early 20th century. N.T. Wright says, "People have been looking for Jesus for a long time, but never quite like this."

Their conclusions differ greatly from what Christian denominations have historically taught. They are also in major conflict with the current beliefs of most present-day conservative Christians.

The initial two hundred scholars has now dwindled to about seventy-four active members who meet periodically to debate newly presented or recently-circulated papers. Among its many recent publications, one stands out as a kind of flagship: The Five Gospels, published late in 1993. It was the book towards which all else was preliminary.

These scholars attempt to reconstruct the life of Jesus. They try to answer who he was, what he did, what he said, and what his sayings meant using all extant evidence and available tools. The Seminar's approach, like that of Funk, is historical and critical, with a strongly skeptical view of traditional Christian belief. http://www.theopedia.com/jesus-seminar

5. Perhaps many of you are thinking you never heard of the Jesus Seminar. Why does it matter?

Almost everything you hear about Jesus and the Bible in the media is influenced by the Jesus Seminar. Every year at Easter and Christmas there will be magazine articles and TV special—all from a very liberal perspective. Most of these are influenced by the Jesus Seminar.

6. What is the goal of the Jesus Seminar?

One group that has been at the forefront of this endeavor calls itself "The Jesus Seminar." Formed in 1985 to examine all the sayings attributed to Jesus in the New Testament and other early Christian documents, the Jesus Seminar has on the surface a simple academic purpose: "to assess the degree of scholarly consensus about the historical authenticity of each of the sayings of Jesus."[1] However, the Jesus Seminar has an agenda other than the academic one—an agenda for the people of the church. This group of scholars has decided "to update and then make the legacy of two hundred years of research and debate a matter of public record."[2] They want to liberate the people of the church from the "dark ages of theological tyranny" by liberating Jesus. As Robert Funk, cofounder of the Jesus Seminar states, "We want to liberate Jesus. The only Jesus most people know is the mythic one. They don't want the real Jesus, they want the one they can worship. The cultic Jesus."

— Jesus *Under Fire: Modern Scholarship Reinvents the Historical Jesus* by Michael J. Wilkins

7. How much of the gospels does the Jesus Seminar accept?

The Seminar's publicity-savvy participants attracted the press by voting with colored beads on whether they thought Jesus said what the gospels quote him as saying. A red bead meant Jesus undoubtedly said this or something like it; a pink bead meant he probably said it; a gray bead meant he didn't say it but the ideas are similar to his own; and a black bead meant he didn't utter these words at all.

In the end they concluded Jesus did not say 82 percent of what the gospels attribute to him. Most of the remaining 18 percent was considered somewhat doubtful, with only 2 percent of Jesus' sayings confidently determined to be authentic. Craving controversy and lacking the expertise to scrutinize the Seminar's methodology, journalists devoted fountains of ink to the story.

Then the Seminar published The Five Gospels, containing the four traditional gospels plus the questionable Gospel of Thomas, with Jesus' words color-coded to match the group's findings. Flip through it and you find expanses of black type but precious little in red. For example, the only words in the Lord's Prayer that the Seminar is convinced Jesus said are "Our Father." — Lee Strobel, *The Case for Christ Movie Edition: Solving the Biggest Mystery of All Time* (Grand Rapids, MI: Zondervan, 2017).

8. **Gregory A. Boyd wrote an interesting book called *Letters From A Skeptic*. It records a series of letters that he and his dad sent back and forth. I'd like to read some of the questions that Boyd's dad asked him and see how you would respond. First: So I'm wondering, where was God when the Christians were slaughtering the Muslims and Jews—women and children included—during the "holy" Crusades? Why did God allow "His people" to burn almost the entire population of Jewish "unbelievers" in Spain during the Spanish Inquisition? Why would an all-loving God allow the church to take part in something like the Holocaust (at best, it looked in the other direction)—and do all these things "in His name"?**

To assume that God is responsible for our evil—even the evil committed "in His name"—is, I suspect, to assume that humans are robots who simply act out a divine, preplanned program. But if that were the case, we could never be loving beings. I want to argue that, ultimately, all evil in the world comes from free wills other than God. What God wills and does is always good. Whatever is not good has its origin from someone or something other than God. The fact that it was the "Christian church" which chose to do the evils you write about, and to do them using God's name, in my mind only serves to show that all that goes under the name of "Christian" is not necessarily Christian. Christianity isn't a religion or an institution of any sort: It's a relationship. Within the religion of Christianity there are, and have always been, genuine Christians—people who have a saving and transforming relationship with Jesus Christ. And this fact accounts for the tremendous good Christianity has brought to the world (in spite of the evils). But the "religion" of Christianity, the "institution" of the church, is not itself Christian. Only people, not institutions, can be Christian. Thus, I want to sharply distinguish between the Christianity I'm defending and the "Christian church": The two need not have anything more than a name in common. I wouldn't dream of trying to defend all that's been done under the label "Christianity." Like you, I am enraged by a great deal of it. — *Letters from a Skeptic: A Son Wrestles with His Father's Questions about Christianity* by Dr. Gregory A. Boyd

9. **But this is really just part of a bigger problem I have with the idea of an all-loving God. It's not just the evil in the church that's the problem, it's the evil in the whole world. If God created this world and cares about it, why is there so damn much suffering in it? In your letter your answer was that God can't be held responsible because He gave man the freedom to choose to do right or wrong. But, Greg, I don't feel that the question can be swept away so easily. When the freedom to decide to do harm results in pain and suffering to innocent people, God is simply not the "loving" God you make Him out to be!**

It seems to me, Dad, that if God is going to give free wills to His creatures, He has to allow for the possibility of them misusing that freedom, even if this means hurting others. To be significantly free is to be morally responsible, and to be morally responsible means being morally responsible to each other. What is the freedom to love or not love unless it is freedom to enrich or harm another? God structured things this way because the alternative would be to have a race of robots who can't genuinely love—but that's hardly worth creating, is it? So why doesn't God intervene every time someone is going to misuse his freedom and hurt another person? The answer, I believe, is found in the nature of freedom itself. A freedom which is prevented from being exercised whenever it was going to be misused simply wouldn't be freedom. Look at it this way: If I give Denay five dollars, can I completely control the way she spends it? If I stepped in every time she was going to spend this money unwisely (according to my judgment), is it really her money at all? Did I really give her anything? If the only things she can buy with her money are things which I decide are worthwhile, is it really her money at all? Is it not rather still my money which I am indirectly spending through her? — *Letters from a Skeptic: A Son Wrestles with His Father's Questions about Christianity* by Dr. Gregory A. Boyd

10. God supposedly is all-knowing, why didn't He just look ahead and see who was and wasn't going to use freedom rightly, and then just create the good people? We'd still have freedom, but in a world without suffering. It strikes me as odd that God should have to take "risks" at all. Isn't He (in your view) in total control?

Your question in your last letter about God's foreknowledge is a good one, but I think it's based on a misconception of what God's omniscience (His knowing everything) entails. In the Christian view God knows all of reality—everything there is to know. But to assume He knows ahead of time how every person is going to freely act assumes that each person's free activity is already there to know—even before he freely does it! But it's not. If we have been given freedom, we create the reality of our decisions by making them. And until we make them, they don't exist. Thus, in my view at least, there simply isn't anything to know until we make it there to know. So God can't foreknow the good or bad decisions of the people He creates until He creates these people and they, in turn, create their decisions. —

Letters from a Skeptic: A Son Wrestles with His Father's Questions about Christianity by Dr. Gregory A. Boyd

11. How do you get God off the hook for evils which don't arise from anyone's decision? Since God is the one who directly creates everything, why does He create famines, earthquakes, mud slides, AIDS, deformed babies, and the like? Surely no one's free will—except God's—can be blamed for these! If He's all-loving, one would think that He'd exercise a little more care with His creation.

In the Christian view, then, the earth has been literally besieged by a power outside itself. There is a power of pure evil which now affects everything and everybody on the earth. The Creator is not the only influence any longer. This is why the earth can be so incredibly beautiful on the one hand, and so incredibly nightmarish on the other. We live, individually and collectively, amidst a contradiction of good and evil. The beauty of the world couldn't be here by indifferent chance, but the evil couldn't be here by good design. (That's what this "problem of evil" is all about.) My claim, then, is that the earth is a battlefield. We are, like Normandy in World War II, caught in the cross fire of a cosmic battle. And on battlefields, as you know, all sorts of terrible things happen. In such a situation, everything becomes a potential weapon, and every person a potential victim. And thus the entire cosmos, the Bible says, is in a state of chaos (Rom. 8). I would never for a moment pretend to understand exactly how these demonic forces screw around with nature—the Bible is completely silent on this score. But it is my deepest conviction that all evil which can't be accounted for by appealing to the necessary limitations of the world or the evil wills of people is due to the will of such beings as these. In the end, we are all more or less casualties of war. —

Letters from a Skeptic: A Son Wrestles with His Father's Questions about Christianity by Dr. Gregory A. Boyd

12. Why would God create Satan in the first place? You'll probably say that it was Satan's free choice to be evil, but if he was created to be so wonderful, how could he make such a bad choice?

The way I think about this matter is as follows. As I wrote in some earlier correspondence, love requires freedom. It must be chosen. And the greater the possibility of love, the greater the possibility of evil. I think we agree on this. But I don't think this implies that love must forever be a tenuous affair. We tend to become the decisions we make. The more we choose something, the more we become that something. We are all in the process of solidifying our identities by the decisions we make. With each decision we make, we pick up momentum in the direction of that decision.

Lucifer, then, was the greatest of all creatures, not because of who he actually was, but because of who he could become. His greatness lay in the magnificent potential for love which he had. But this also implied that he had an unthinkable potential for evil. And a decision started the difference. The difference between a Hitler and a Mother Teresa started somewhere with a small decision. — *Letters from a Skeptic: A Son Wrestles with His Father's Questions about Christianity* by Dr. Gregory A. Boyd

13. Is your God all-powerful?

Is my God all-powerful? I want to answer yes and no. Let me explain myself. It is my view (which I believe to be biblical) that God is all-powerful in the sense that God originally possessed all power. Before Creation, God was the only being who existed, and thus had all the power there was. He could do anything, and nothing opposed Him. But with the creation of free creatures, I maintain, God necessarily surrendered a degree of His power. Or perhaps it is better to say God delegated some of His power. Our freedom is a little piece of "controlling power" lent us by God. In order to allow creatures to be free, then, God voluntarily gives us a portion of His power, and thereby surrenders His opportunity to "always get His way." I don't think it could be any other way, for freedom must entail that the free person can decide his own way—and it may not agree with God's way. It is utterly impossible for God to be always in control and yet allow free beings to exercise some control. Thus, to the extent that God "lends" power away, He no longer utilizes it. However, what's important to realize, Dad, is that this "surrender" of control is completely a voluntary act of God. If there is "limit" on God's power, it is only there by His decision, not some power outside of Himself. — *Letters from a Skeptic: A Son Wrestles with His Father's Questions about Christianity* by Dr. Gregory A. Boyd

14. Why believe in God in the first place?

So, for example, we humans instinctively assume that reality should be rational, and that reasoning gets us closer to truth (and science seems to say that this assumption is valid), but in the end nature is irrational. There is no overarching mind to it. We humans instinctively assume that love is a reality, that it is the only ideal worth living for and dying for. But nature seems to be an indifferent, loveless, brute process of colliding chemicals—and so our ideals are reduced to reacting hormones. We humans instinctively assume that our moral convictions are true to reality, do we not? There are, of course, people who say that moral convictions are "just a matter of taste," but cut them off at an intersection and their convictions change. You did a gross injustice! And we humans instinctively hunger for meaning and purpose. You can see it all around in the way people behave. We strive to infuse our lives with some sort of significance, some sort of meaning. But if our cosmos is ultimately indifferent and purposeless, all we are, all we do, all we believe in, all we strive for is "dust in the wind." After we exist, it matters not whether anyone has ever, or ever will again exist. Everything is ultimately meaningless. So, unless the ultimate source of all existence is at least as personal as we are, Dad, my contention is that who we are is both unexplainable and extremely hard to swallow. — *Letters from a Skeptic: A Son Wrestles with His Father's Questions about Christianity* by Dr. Gregory A. Boyd

15. You then say that humans aren't explainable unless there's a personal being who created us, but couldn't we just have come about by accident? Isn't that what the biologists tell us? Doesn't evolutionary theory say that our minds and morality are just part of our survival drive? I'm not even sure what I think about the theory itself, but it's an alternative explanation.

I'd say the exact same thing about morality. If morality is simply the result of chance, what a certain species of primates needed to help them survive, then our moral claims have no objective reference point. They don't say anything about the way things are, only about the way we (by accident of evolution) feel. But when you say that Hitler was "wrong" for slaughtering six million Jews, or when you say that that lunatic guy you wrote me about was "wrong" for mutilating that girl, you mean more than just "you don't like how it feels." Don't you assume that these deeds contradict the way things ought to be? Aren't you making a claim not about the way you are, but about the way the universe is? Aren't you assuming there is a moral law in the universe, in the very structure of things, which these idiots have violated? What is very important to see, however, is that chance, sheer chemical reactions, can be no more moral than they can be rational. And since the effect cannot be greater than the cause, the "force" which lies behind the cosmos must not only be rational: It must be moral. And now the "it" is starting to look a whole lot like a person.

Let me say one final word, Dad, about why I believe in God. I really do feel that this argument (and many others like it) is valid. In a sense, I feel like it is simply consistently drawing out the implications of what all of us believe about ourselves and the world anyway. But my belief in God isn't a mere theory which I happen to hold to be true. It is a relationship. When I came to believe in God, and came to trust in the sacrifice of Jesus Christ as the only way I could be made right with this "moral force" I must someday answer to, I discovered by experience that the longings of personhood do have "an answer." I was a dried-up fish that discovered there actually was water! And what wonderful, refreshing, and fulfilling water it was! All that the heart longs for is not only given an explanation by a faith in God: They are given their fulfillment. My hope, Dad, is that someday you will not only agree with my theory, but share in this relationship. — *Letters from a Skeptic: A Son Wrestles with His Father's Questions about Christianity* by Dr. Gregory A. Boyd

16. When Arlyle was dying, we all prayed till we were blue in the face. Even you kids prayed. Maybe God doesn't listen to the prayers of sinful adults, but He should have at least heard the cries of you kids! Instead, you kids were left motherless and that set in motion a rather unfortunate history you yourself know only too well. If God had been personally concerned about us, Greg, He'd have spared your mother and spared all of us a tremendous amount of pain. You can try to explain this, I suppose, with your cosmic warfare theory, but it seems easier to simply conclude that He doesn't give a damn.

Like every kid, I grew up with a need to feel unconditional love and acceptance from a mom, but this I never felt. As you know, sometimes we kids got the opposite message from our stepmother.1 I always knew you loved me—and I remember always feeling "safe" when you came home—but your job took you away from the home most of the time. So, looking back on it, I can see that I grew up with an acute sense of abandonment. The full force of the pain of this didn't even hit me until I was an adult. Kids block out what they cannot bear. But around the age of 20, after being a Christian for about three years, I received something that was far more important than an answer to my question "why": I received healing (and I'm still receiving it). Many memories from my childhood began coming back to me—usually in times of prayer—and they were sometimes extremely painful. I was, I guess, now healthy enough to deal with them. But in the face of these the Lord brought love and healing. In the face of many of the things I interpreted as a kid as being a negative commentary on my self-worth (e.g., some of my stepmother's aberrant forms of punishment), the Lord showed me that I am loveable and infinitely precious in His eyes. And He caused me to experience this. In the face of the abandonment I experienced, the Lord said to me, "I will never leave you or forsake you" (Heb. 13:5). And in the face of my need for the unconditionally loving mother I never had, the Lord said, "I want to be that mother to you." And "He" is! Christ isn't our adversary in times of suffering: He's our cure. Christ became that for me. My soul was, and is, filled with the unconditional love of Jesus. And unconditional love is the only life source for the soul and the only medicine for its wounds. An intellectual answer could never do that. My question still remains, but Christ has won my trust in Him by showing me His beauty—the beauty of a love, a grace, a tenderness, a gentle strength which no mere human being could ever match. He won my love and trust through the healing compassion of His eyes and the warm understanding of His embrace. He provided an understanding in the heart which the mind could never grasp. (That's why the Bible says that God gives believers a "peace that passes all understanding.") What I also experienced, Dad, and what is shown throughout the New Testament, is that Jesus suffers with us in our suffering. That's how He heals us of our suffering. One of His names in the New Testament is "Immanuel," which means "God is with us." However low we sink, God is with us. He's there at the bottom waiting for us! He isn't off on some distant planet, indifferent to our plight. He's in the midst of all we go through.

Only the gospel dares to proclaim that God enters smack-dab into the middle of the hell we create. Only the gospel dares to proclaim that God was born a baby in a bloody, crap-filled stable, that He lived a life befriending the prostitutes and lepers no one else would befriend, and that He suffered, firsthand, the hellish depth of all that is nightmarish in human existence. Only the gospel portrait of God makes sense of the contradictory fact that the world is at once so beautiful and so ugly. — *Letters from a Skeptic: A Son Wrestles with His Father's Questions about Christianity* by Dr. Gregory A. Boyd

17. Why trust the Gospel accounts?

So it is with the Gospels, Dad. I'm not asking you to accept on "blind faith" that they are God's Word. Forget about that altogether for right now. I'm simply saying, look at them as you would any ancient document. Apply to them the same criteria historians apply to other ancient documents when they research history. And my contention is that, when the Gospels are treated in this critical-historical way, they fare very well and can be trusted to tell us a good deal about the person of Jesus Christ, enough, in fact, to know that God was present in Him and working through Him in a most significant way. — *Letters from a Skeptic: A Son Wrestles with His Father's Questions about Christianity* by Dr. Gregory A. Boyd

18. How can you believe that a man rose from the dead?

First, you hold that the resurrection is simply "an article of faith" that one simply believes or doesn't. So you suspect we've hit a stalemate. I don't agree. Of course a belief in the resurrection is more than a theoretical hypothesis about a historical event, but this doesn't mean that it has nothing to do with a hypothesis about a historical event. The event took place in history, and thus it must be ascertained by historical criteria, just like any other supposed historical event. It takes more than evidence to believe in the resurrection of Christ—I believe it also takes the Spirit of God working in a person's heart—but this doesn't mean that this belief can or should be held apart from historical evidence. When it comes to truth, the mind and the Spirit work in harmony. — *Letters from a Skeptic: A Son Wrestles with His Father's Questions about Christianity* by Dr. Gregory A. Boyd

19. How can you believe that a man was God?

Now, is the belief that Jesus embodies God's presence in human form a contradiction, as you suggest? On what basis can anyone maintain this? It would be a contradiction only if being God by definition ruled out being human, and vice versa. But do we know enough, through our own little reason, about the nature of God, or the nature of humans, to conclude this? I think not. The only way we could know the nature of God is by God Himself telling us, and all the evidence suggests that Jesus Christ is just the place where this "telling" is done. The incarnation is, I grant, paradoxical, for we cannot understand how it is true. But it is not contradictory, for it is not nonsense to hold that it is true. The analogy that is frequently used by theologians is that physicists say something similar about the nature of light. It can be proven that light has both wave- and particle-like features. But this is paradoxical, for we have no way of conceiving how something could have both of these features simultaneously. But since the evidence for both features is incontrovertible, physicists yet assert that it is, in fact, true. — *Letters from a Skeptic: A Son Wrestles with His Father's Questions about Christianity* by Dr. Gregory A. Boyd

20. How can another man's death pardon me?

To be perfectly up front with you, Dad, I really don't know how this occurs. The church has never arrived at any definite theology of how we are made right with God through the work of the cross (what's called "the atonement"). I don't think we should be too surprised at this, however. If we find the fundamental structure of physical reality to be impervious to our reason—science is increasingly arriving at just this conclusion—should we find it surprising if the central act whereby God redeems the world is also clouded in mystery? I think not. Nevertheless, there are two things which I'd like to say which might clear up the matter for you somewhat. First, Dad, it's important to realize that Jesus was not just "a man" whose death 2,000 years ago gets you off the hook. Jesus was not an innocent "third party" that God punished in place of us. Rather, Jesus is Himself God as well as man. He is not only the one judged for the crime; He is the one against whom the crime is committed, and the one who passes out the sentence for the crime. The Judge Himself became the judged! So there is no "third party" in this transaction, Dad. There are only two parties—the all-holy God and sinful humanity—and the Jesus who died for us is both. This is not injustice, Dad; this is incomprehensible love. Secondly, without trying to explain exactly how the atonement occurred, or whether it had to happen the way it did, I think we are given enough insight in Scripture to make sense of the fact that it occurred the way it did. We can say why Jesus died for us without going so far as to say that He had to die for us. — *Letters from a Skeptic: A Son Wrestles with His Father's Questions about Christianity* by Dr. Gregory A. Boyd

21. How can I be sure it's all true?

So, there is always a "leap" involved in believing anything. But what I want you to see, Dad, is that you are already taking this "leap." A person who chooses not to believe, or even just to suspend judgment, is taking a tremendous risk, a tremendous "leap of faith," for he may be wrong, and this may have severe consequences for him. It's like being in a house and someone outside hollers "fire"! You can choose to believe him or not to believe him—and you weigh the evidence carefully (do you smell smoke? do you see flames? etc.). You can choose to believe and risk looking foolish for running out of your house if it's a joke, or you can choose not to believe and risk being burned up. If you choose to suspend judgment, you risk the same thing. So there simply is no "risk-free" position, not even the position of not taking a position. — *Letters from a Skeptic: A Son Wrestles with His Father's Questions about Christianity* by Dr. Gregory A. Boyd

22. What impressed you about Gregory Boyd's responses?

23. How can we pray for each other this week?

Case for Christ / Lesson #7 / Chapter 7
Was Jesus Really Convinced That He Was the Son of God?
Good Questions Have Groups Talking
www.joshhunt.com

DIG

1. **State your name and… If you could ask Lee Strobel one question, what would it be?**

2. **Who read Chapter 7 this week? What got your attention?**

3. **This week's interview is with Ben Witherington III. What is his expertise? What do you recall about him?**

    This topic is familiar territory to Witherington, whose books include The Christology of Jesus, Jesus the Sage, The Many Faces of the Christ, The Jesus Quest, Jesus, Paul, and the End of the World, Reading and Understanding the Bible, New Testament History, and commentaries on Mark, John, Acts, and Romans. His articles have been featured in specialized dictionaries and academic journals. — Lee Strobel, *The Case for Christ Movie Edition: Solving the Biggest Mystery of All Time* (Grand Rapids, MI: Zondervan, 2017).

4. **How did Jesus see Himself? Did Jesus see himself as God?**

    Perhaps no claim is more direct than Jesus' response to Caiaphas's point-blank interrogation:

"Are you the Christ, the Son of the Blessed One?"

"I am," said Jesus. "And you will see the Son of Man sitting at the right hand of the Mighty One and coming on the clouds of heaven."

The high priest tore his clothes. "Why do we need any more witnesses?" he asked. "You have heard the blasphemy. What do you think?" They all condemned him as worthy of death (Mark 14:61–64).

Notice that Jesus responded to the direct question with a direct answer: "I am." Referring to himself as the "Son of Man," Jesus then added that he would be coming back on the clouds of heaven. Caiaphas and his onlookers knew the implication. This was a reference to the vision the Old Testament prophet Daniel had of the end times: the Messiah—the Son of Man—will come to earth to judge the world on the authority given to him by God the Father ("the Ancient of Days"), and all the world's people will worship him (Dan. 7:13). Of course, no one is to be worshiped but God himself. Yet here was Christ claiming that he would be the one to judge the world and receive worship from its people. He was claiming to be God, and everyone knew it. — Norman L. Geisler and Frank Turek, *I Don't Have Enough Faith to Be an Atheist* (Wheaton, IL: Crossway Books, 2004), 340–341.

5. Why wasn't Jesus more explicit in his declaration of Himself as God?

"The truth is that Jesus was a bit mysterious about his identity, wasn't he?" I asked as Witherington pulled up a chair across from me. "He tended to shy away from forthrightly proclaiming himself to be the Messiah or the Son of God. Was that because he didn't think of himself in those terms or because he had other reasons?"

"No, it's not because he didn't think of himself in those terms," Witherington said as he settled into his chair and crossed his legs. "If he had simply announced, 'Hi, folks; I'm God,' that would have been heard as 'I'm Yahweh,' because the Jews of his day didn't have any concept of the Trinity. They only knew of God the Father—whom they called Yahweh—and not God the Son or God the Holy Spirit.

"So if someone were to say he was God, that wouldn't have made any sense to them and would have been seen as clear-cut blasphemy. And it would have been counterproductive to Jesus in his efforts to get people to listen to his message.

"Besides, there were already a host of expectations about what the Messiah would look like, and Jesus didn't want to be pigeonholed into somebody else's categories. Consequently, he was very careful about what he said publicly. In private with his disciples—that was a different story, but the gospels primarily tell us about what he did in public." — Lee Strobel, *The Case for Christ Movie Edition: Solving the Biggest Mystery of All Time* (Grand Rapids, MI: Zondervan, 2017).

6. Luke 11.14 – 20. What does this passage tell us about how Jesus saw himself?

Again I interrupted. "Elaborate on that a bit," I said. "How does it set him apart?"

"Jesus sees his miracles as bringing about something unprecedented—the coming of God's dominion," replied Witherington. "He doesn't merely see himself as a worker of miracles; he sees himself as the one in whom and through whom the promises of God come to pass. And that's a not-too-thinly-veiled claim of transcendence." — Lee Strobel, *The Case for Christ*

Movie Edition: Solving the Biggest Mystery of All Time (Grand Rapids, MI: Zondervan, 2017).

7. How does this passage reveal Jesus' deity?

Then he adds, "But if I drive out demons by the finger of God, then the kingdom of God has come upon you" (v. 20). When asked by some of John the Baptist's followers, after their master had been thrown into prison, whether he is the Messiah, Jesus replies, "Go back and report to John what you have seen and heard: the blind receive sight, the lame walk, those who have leprosy are cleansed, the deaf hear, the dead are raise...." (Luke 7:22 par.). In other words, the miracles point to Jesus's messiahship. If the kingdom has arrived, then its king must be present. If the Messiah has come, then the messianic age must be at hand. The specific kinds of miracles prophesied in Isaiah 35:5–6 were being fulfilled. Similar conclusions about Jesus's identity can be derived from Mark 2:10–11, as Jesus provides forgiveness of sins while healing the paralyzed man lowered to him through a hole dug in the flat roof, and from Jesus's words just before the raising of Lazarus, in which he declares himself to be "the resurrection and the life" (John 11:25). — Craig Blomberg, *Can We Still Believe the Bible? An Evangelical Engagement with Contemporary Questions* (Grand Rapids, MI: Baker, 2014), 202.

8. John 8.58. What do we learn about the way Jesus saw Himself from this passage?

The hypostatic union is the term used to describe how God the Son, Jesus Christ, took on a human nature, yet remained fully God at the same time. Jesus always had been God (John 8:58, 10:30), but at the incarnation Jesus became a human being (John 1:14). The addition of the human nature to the divine nature is Jesus, the God-man. This is the hypostatic union, Jesus Christ, one Person, fully God and fully man. — Got Questions Ministries, *Got Questions? Bible Questions Answered* (Bellingham, WA: Logos Bible Software, 2002–2013).

9. What does Jesus say, "I am," not, "I was"?

If there had been any doubt about what Jesus meant in his other "I am" revelations, the confusion was cleared up in the conversations recorded in John 8 and 10. The Jews understood exactly what Jesus was saying, and they wanted to kill him for it. As Jesus taught in the temple courtyard, the religious leaders challenged his earlier statements about himself. In the exchange that followed, Jesus told the Pharisees that whoever obeyed his words would never die.

At this remark, the Jews accused Jesus of being demon possessed. Abraham and the prophets had died; did Jesus think he was greater than them? Jesus told the Jews that their ancestor Abraham had joyfully looked forward to Jesus's day. They demanded to know how Jesus could possibly have seen Abraham, who had lived two thousand years earlier. His answer stunned them: "Before Abraham was ever born, I am" (8:58).

These Jews were familiar with the passage in Exodus where God spoke with Moses from a burning bush. When Moses asked whom he should say had sent him to the Israelites, God answered, "I Am Who I Am" (3:14). He instructed Moses to say that "I Am" had sent him. Jesus used the equivalent of that Hebrew expression, applying God's holy name to himself. The Jews picked up stones to carry out the death penalty prescribed in Leviticus 24:16 for anyone blaspheming and claiming to be God.

Anyone familiar with the Bible cannot ignore Jesus's claims of deity. Such statements demand a response from us. We can react like the unbelieving Jews and be stunned by the audacity of what we see as outlandish assertions. Or we can take Jesus at his word and worship him as the eternal God, the same One who spoke from a burning bush to Moses and who later taught in the temple courts. While Abraham looked ahead to Jesus's day with joy, we can look backward and rejoice that "I Am" came to earth to die for our sins. — Dianne Neal Matthews, *Designed for Devotion: A 365-Day Journey from Genesis to Revelation* (Grand Rapids, MI: Baker, 2012).

10. John 5.24 – 30. What does Jesus reveal about Himself from this passage?

The clearest of Jesus' spoken claims to deity found anywhere in the New Testament come in John's Gospel, chapter five.

He was God in the form of a human being: John 5:17–18

He had power to raise the dead: John 5:21, 28–29

He would be the future judge of all people: John 5:22

He claimed equal honor with God: John 5:23

He was able to give life to people, in place of death: John 5:24

WHAT'S THE CONCLUSION?

The question which Jesus asked his disciples, "Who do you say I am?" (Matthew 16:15), is the query we have to answer. The best place to find the answer is within the pages of the four Gospels.

We're not responsible for what leading theologians believe. In many ways they have divergent views about

Jesus, just as the leading theologians had in Jesus' own day. We are responsible, though, to come to a firm conclusion of whether we believe or disbelieve the claims about Jesus. — Mark Water, *Hard Questions about Christianity Made Easy, The Made Easy Series* (Alresford, Hampshire: John Hunt Publishing, 2000), 35.

11. By the way, does verse 29 suggest we are saved by works?

First, Jesus does not believe in salvation by works. In the beginning of John's Gospel, John writes, "But as many as received Him, to them He gave the right to become children of God, even to those who believe in His name: who were born, not of blood, nor of the will of the flesh, nor of the will of man, but of God" (John 1:12–13). Jesus says in John 3:16–18:

For God so loved the world that He gave His only begotten Son, that whoever believes in Him should not perish but have everlasting life.

For God did not send His Son into the world to condemn the world, but that the world through Him might be saved. He who believes in Him is not condemned; but he who does not believe is condemned already, because he has not believed in the name of the only begotten Son of God.

Furthermore, in John 5:24, Jesus says, "Truly, truly, I say to you, he who hears My word, and believes Him who sent Me, has eternal life" (NASB). From these passages it is clear that Jesus did not believe in works salvation.

Second, Jesus' reference to good works in John 5:28–29 is to that which occurs after saving faith. To be saved, one needs the grace of God (Eph. 2:8–9), but authentic faith expresses itself in good works (v. 10). The Apostle

Paul in the Book of Romans, says something very similar to what Jesus says in John 5:28–29. In Romans Paul says that God "will render to every man according to his deeds: to those who by perseverance in doing good seek for glory and honor and immortality, eternal life; but to those who are selfishly ambitious and do not obey the truth, but obey unrighteousness, wrath and indignation" (Rom. 2:6–8, NASB). But Paul also wrote, "For by grace you have been saved through faith, and that not of yourselves; it is the gift of God" (Eph. 2:8). In the passage in Romans, Paul is not talking about the one who obtains eternal life by faith, but the individual who shows this life in his good works. In Ephesians, Paul is saying that none can save himself by works prior to salvation. (See also comments on James 2:21.)

So, Jesus does not contradict Himself nor the rest of Scripture concerning the matter of salvation. Those who receive the resurrection of life have shown their saving faith by their works. — Norman L. Geisler and Thomas A. Howe, *When Critics Ask : A Popular Handbook on Bible Difficulties* (Wheaton, Ill.: Victor Books, 1992), 409.

12. Back up and look at John 5.16 – 23. What do we learn about Jesus from this passage?

Jesus was either God in human form, or a crackpot. There is no middle ground. In verses 17–29 He said:

- Whatever He saw the Father do, He did.

- God showed Jesus everything He did and He had even greater things to show Him, which would cause the people to be astonished.

- Just as God raised the dead and gave life to them, so Jesus gives life to whoever He would.

- God Himself had appointed Jesus of Nazareth as the Judge of all mankind.

- Humanity should honor Jesus as much as they honor the Father.

- Those who didn't honor Jesus didn't honor God.

- All who heard His words and trusted in the Father escape the wrath of the Law.

- All who trusted Him passed from death to life.

- The hour would come when everyone in their graves would hear the voice of Jesus, and be raised from the dead.

- As God is the source of all life, so He has given Jesus life in Himself.

Ray Comfort, *The Evidence Bible: Irrefutable Evidence for the Thinking Mind, Notes, ed. Kirk Cameron, The Way of the Master Evidence Bible* (Orlando, FL: Bridge-Logos, 2003), 1351.

13. How does this passage affirm Jesus' claim to deity?

Christ's answer to the Pharisees' charge that he claimed to be equal with God reinforced that claim with four statements (each beginning with for [gar in the original]):

1. in the equal relationship between the father and the son (5:19), whatever one does, the other does as well;

2. the love between the father and the son gives rise to mighty works (5:20);

3. the son shares the father's power to give life—both spiritual and physical resurrection (5:21); and

4. the son will judge all men (5:22).

That kind of omnipotence can take care of all impotence. Jesus Christ is, indeed, Lord of all. — Charles C. Ryrie, *The Miracles of Our Lord* (Dubuque, IA: ECS Ministries, 2005), 27.

14. Matthew 25.31 – 33. Jesus' favorite term for Himself was "Son of Man." What does Jesus reveal about Himself from this passage?

When the Son of Man comes in his glory. The final parable (or judgment scene) of the Eschatological Discourse is set at the time of final judgment. By referring to the Son of Man (the King) coming in glory as judge over all the nations, Matthew evokes Daniel 7:13–14 in the Septuagint and highlights the universal authority that Jesus as Son of Man will exercise (see 28:18). — Jeannine K. Brown, *Matthew*, ed. Mark L. Strauss and John H. Walton, *Teach the Text Commentary Series* (Grand Rapids, MI: Baker Books, 2015), 287.

15. How is this picture of Jesus different from what we celebrate at Christmas?

Let us mark in the first place, who will be the Judge in the last day. We read that it will be "the Son of Man," Jesus Christ Himself.

That same Jesus who was born in the manger of Bethlehem, and took upon Him the form of a servant,—who was despised and rejected of men, and often had not where to lay His head,—who was condemned by the princes of this world, beaten, scourged, and nailed to the cross,—that same Jesus shall Himself judge the world, when He comes in His glory. To Him the Father hath committed all judgment. (John 5:22.) To Him at last every knee shall bow, and every tongue confess that He is Lord. (Philip. 2:10, 11.)

Let believers think of this, and take comfort. He that sits upon the throne in that great and dreadful day will be their Saviour, their Shepherd, their High Priest, their elder Brother, their Friend. When they see Him, they will have no cause to be alarmed.

Let unconverted people think of this, and be afraid. Their judge will be that very Christ, whose Gospel they now despise, and whose gracious invitations they refuse to hear. How great will be their confusion at last, if they go on in unbelief and die in their sins! To be condemned in the day of judgment by any one would be awful. But to be condemned by Him who would have saved them will be awful indeed. Well may the Psalmist say, "Kiss the Son lest he be angry." (Psalm 2:12.) — J. C. Ryle, *Expository Thoughts on Matthew* (New York: Robert Carter & Brothers, 1860), 341.

16. John 2.19 – 22. How does this passage affirm Jesus claim to deity?

The Greek word translated "temple" is naos, which was also used in reference to the Holy of Holies. Perhaps Jesus physically pointed to Himself when He made this declaration. At the very least, He alluded to Himself when He made it. "Destroy this temple—Me," He said, "and in three days I will raise it up"—which is precisely what happened at Calvary. — Jon Courson, *Jon Courson's Application Commentary* (Nashville, TN: Thomas Nelson, 2003), 453.

17. How was Jesus' body like the temple in Jerusalem?

Some words that Jesus used here could be used in connection with either a physical body or a brick building. Jesus was comparing his body to the amazing temple in Jerusalem. Remember that the temple was the place to which people could go to meet God. So Jesus was strongly hinting that he was the one through whom people could come to meet God.

That's why he said, 'Destroy this temple, and I will raise it again in three days.' This, of course, was precisely what happened. Jesus was crucified on a cross three years later outside the city walls of Jerusalem and rose from the dead on the third day. And later, as they looked back, the disciples saw the full significance of these words. — Andrew Paterson, *Opening Up John's Gospel, Opening Up Commentary* (Leominster: Day One Publications, 2010), 25–26.

18. John 20.28. How does this passage reveal Jesus' deity?

Faced with irrefutable proof that Jesus had been bodily raised from the dead, he concluded that Jesus was God. The Greek text is quite clear that Thomas was addressing Jesus when he said unto him, "My Lord and my God!"

This passage is without a doubt where Arianism meets its greatest defeat. The Greek text is free from variant readings. The word ὁ θεός has the definite article in front of it. The phrase is introduced by the words "he said unto Him" (εἶπεν αὐτῷ) which means that the statement "My Lord and my God!" is addressed to Jesus. The grammar of the Greek is clear. The form of address is in the vocative case. Robertson even uses John 20:28 as an example of the vocative in his Greek grammar and concludes:

When Thomas said Ὁ κύριός μου καὶ ὁ θεός μου (John 20:28), he gave Christ full acceptance of his deity and of the fact of his resurrection. — Robert A. Morey, *The Trinity: Evidence and Issues* (Iowa Falls, IA: World Pub., 1996), 328–329.

19. What are we to conclude? Did Jesus see Himself as God?

Jesus' critics say He was a great, moral teacher but He never claimed to be God. They argue that His followers created the legend of His deity after He was gone. That charge raises several questions: What did Jesus say about Himself? What difference does it make if He said He was God? What alternatives remain about His identity if He was not God?

A person who declares himself God reduces the options as to what he truly is. If he's not God only two alternatives are possible. First, he could be nuts, a lunatic. Many people in mental hospitals and a few on the street claim deity, but their lives and character soon reveal otherwise. Jesus' life and character, however, support His claim. Second, he could be a deceiver, a deliberate liar. Religious charlatans are common, but they're eventually exposed as frauds. Jesus' miracles, good deeds, and sacrificial life argue that He was genuine. But did He say He was God? The Gospels record three kinds of evidence that reveal Jesus' belief in His own deity.

First, He directly said so. Consider John 8:58: "Before Abraham was born, I am!" This alleges more than prior existence—"I am" was the special name God gave to identify Himself when talking to Moses in Exodus 3:14. Those who heard Jesus use it thought He was claiming deity because they took up rocks to stone Him—the punishment for blasphemy. He also admitted His deity in Luke 22:70 during His trial for His life: "They all asked, 'Are you then the Son of God?' He replied, 'You are right in saying I am.'"

Second, He said and did several things to equate Himself with God. For instance, in John 5:17-18 He presumed a special relationship, "He was even calling God his own Father, making himself equal with God." He also modified God's law: "You have heard that it was said … But I tell you …." (Matthew 5:21-22); and, "Heaven and earth will pass away, but my words will never pass away" (Matthew 24:35). Furthermore, He declared Himself the only way to God in John 14:6: "I am the way and the truth and the life. No one comes to the Father except through me." He even forgave sins: "Then Jesus said to her, 'Your sins are forgiven'" (Luke 7:48); and He claimed to be the final judge in eternity: "The Father … has entrusted all judgment to the Son" (John 5:22).

Third, He accepted others' statements of His deity including their worship, "When they saw him, they worshiped him" (Matthew 28:17); their prayer, "You may ask me for anything in my name, and I will do it" (John 14:14); and their direct admission of His deity, "Then those who were in the boat worshiped him, saying, 'Truly you are the Son of God'" (Matthew 14:33).

Jesus saw Himself as deity, the One through whom God entered the human race and through whom God spoke and acted. Could He be wrong? That's highly unlikely given the evidence of His miracles and resurrection. We can be sure of one thing—He did see Himself as God, and if He was not, He was no great, moral teacher. He left us only three options: He was either a raving lunatic, a devious liar, or the Lord of the universe. Whoever we believe He is sets the path of our life and our eternity.

— Rick Cornish, *5 Minute Apologist: Maximum Truth in Minimum Time* (Colorado Springs, CO: NavPress, 2014).

20. How can we pray for each other this week?

Case for Christ / Lesson #8 / Chapter 8
Was Jesus Crazy When He Claimed to Be God?
Good Questions Have Groups Talking
www.joshhunt.com

DIG

1. **State your name and… If you could ask Lee Strobel one question, what would it be?**

2. **Who read Chapter 8 this week? What got your attention?**

3. **Let's review. Isn't the whole Christian religion based on some old stories in old books that are myths that modern science has debunked? How do we know what Jesus really said? How do we know He performed miracles? How do we know He rose from the dead? How do we know He founded a Church? How do we know Jesus even existed? Only because we assume that the Bible is true. But the existence of Jesus is only an idea, an opinion, a belief. It may be true or it may be false, but it's only an opinion, not a fact. And it's also an old idea or opinion, a prescientific idea.**

    There are four mistakes in this argument.

    a. The first mistake is the most important one. Our faith is not based on human ideas or opinions. It is based on the reality of God. God is not an idea any more than you are. The reality of God is a fact, just as much as the reality of you is a fact. God is not real because we believe in Him; we believe in Him because He is real. You are not real because your friend believes in you; your friend believes in you because you are real.

(Of course, the way your friend knows you are real is not the same as the way you know God is real. Your friend can see you, but you can't see God, because you are confined to a physical body, and God is not.)

b. The second mistake is the assumption that old ideas cannot be just as reliable as new ideas. In fact, old ideas can be even more reliable, for they have stood the test of time.

You can't find out whether an idea is true or false just by finding out whether it's old or new. Some old ideas are true, and some are false. Some new ideas are true, and some are false. You don't tell the truth by a calendar or a clock.

In fact, if you think all old ideas are false just because they're old, that makes you a kind of snob. A snob is someone who feels superior to another class of people and is prejudiced against them. If it's stupid to be prejudiced against some class of people in the present, then it's also stupid to be prejudiced against all people in the past. If it's stupid to be a snob, it's also stupid to be a historical snob.

c. The third mistake is the assumption that the historical stories in the Bible are myths, like fairy tales. They are not. They are historical accounts handed down from eyewitnesses. People saw the Red Sea part; people saw Jesus perform miracles.

People who do not believe miracles can ever happen often interpret the Bible's miracle stories as myths instead of facts. But that's confusing interpretation with belief. What you believe is dependent on you; your beliefs are your ideas. But your interpretation of someone else's words should be dependent on that other person's ideas. Interpretation means trying to find out what the other person meant, not what you would have meant. The authors of the Bible are trying to communicate their ideas to you. Listen!

The miracle stories in the Bible cannot be interpreted as myths because they claim to be facts. The Bible explicitly says they are not myths: "For we did not follow cleverly devised myths when we made known to you the power and coming of our Lord Jesus Christ, but we were eyewitnesses of his majesty" (2 Pet 1:16). The Gospels are either deliberate lies or facts. These events either happened, or they didn't. If they happened, they are facts. If they didn't, then the Bible's claims that they did is a lie.

This is especially true of Jesus' Resurrection. First Corinthians 15:14, 17 says: "If Christ has not been raised, then our preaching is in vain and your faith is in vain.... If Christ has not been raised, your faith is futile and you are still in your sins."

d. The fourth mistake is the assumption that our faith begins with the Bible. You don't have to prove the Bible is true first, and then prove from the Bible that the Church is true, and then prove from the Church that Jesus is true, and then prove from Jesus that God is true. It's the other way around. You start with God. You believe in Jesus because He is God. You believe in the Church because she is Jesus' Church. You believe in the Bible because it is the Church's book. — Peter J. Kreeft, *Because God Is Real: Sixteen Questions, One Answer* (San Francisco: Ignatius Press, 2008), 61–63.

4. But wasn't the Bible written in an old, prescientific style, the style of myth?

No, most of it was not. The Bible is different from all other religious literature because it records historical facts, real events that were actually seen by eyewitnesses. It is simply a literary fact that most of the Bible, especially the Gospels, has a very different literary style than the pagan myths. You can see that for yourself by comparing the two.

Actually, the word "myth" can be used in at least three different ways, and we should distinguish these three meanings when we speak about the Bible.

a. When we say of something that it's a "myth", we often mean simply that it's not true, that it's a lie that some people are "suckered into" and deceived by—for instance, the myth that the ancient Roman emperors were gods, or that Communism was a political system that helped the poor, or that George Washington once threw a silver dollar across the Potomac River.

b. At other times, we mean by a "myth" something that's not literally true but is symbolically true. It's not meant to be a lie or a deception. For instance, Aesop's fables, stories about talking animals, are myths. Animals don't really talk, and Aesop doesn't try to deceive us into thinking that they do, but his stories use the myth of talking animals to teach true moral principles. So do many other children's stories about talking animals.

c. Sometimes, even real historical events can be told in mythic, symbolic, nonliteral language. When we say "George Washington was the father of his country", we don't mean it literally, physically, biologically. We use symbolic language. We often do this even when we narrate real historical events. — Peter J. Kreeft,

Because God Is Real: Sixteen Questions, One Answer (San Francisco: Ignatius Press, 2008), 64–65.

5. But the Bible was written by primitive people who didn't know modern science. How can we trust it?

If the Bible claimed to be a science textbook, it would indeed be a primitive one. But that is not its purpose.

The Bible does, however, speak about real people, places, and events. It makes many claims about historical events that can be checked out by science—more than any other religious book does. Other religious books, like the scriptures of Hinduism, Buddhism, or Islam, mention very few historical events. They teach timeless theological truths (or, perhaps, falsehoods) and moral principles and speak of private religious and mystical experiences, but science can't prove or disprove any of those, because science can prove or disprove only historical facts. The Bible mentions thousands of historical facts, and science has never refuted a single one. — Peter J. Kreeft, *Because God Is Real: Sixteen Questions, One Answer* (San Francisco: Ignatius Press, 2008), 61–63.

6. But the Bible is only a book, after all, not a historical fact. How can we trust it?

Books are historical facts too, just as much as the people who write them.

Books are humanity's most reliable way of passing information down through time and across space.

Both the Bible and Jesus are called the "Word of God". The Bible is the Word of God on paper; Jesus is the Word of God in flesh.

A person is more than a book, and Jesus is more than the Bible. A book points to a person, and the Bible points to Jesus. — Peter J. Kreeft, *Because God Is Real: Sixteen Questions, One Answer* (San Francisco: Ignatius Press, 2008), 61–63.

7. **But the Bible writers were writing to people who were ignorant of the facts of history. They were gullible: they could believe anything.**

This is an example of "historical snobbery". (See page 62.) It is simply not true. Most cultures in the past took their history much more seriously than we do. They preserved and treasured and remembered their history with great care. Many people today are much more gullible and ignorant of history than the people in Bible times were. For instance, many people who read Dan Brown's novel The Da Vinci Code believe that this piece of fiction could have been historical fact. They believe the ridiculous ideas that this novel presents as real history: for instance, that none of Jesus' followers for the first three hundred years believed that Jesus was divine until the emperor Constantine invented the idea in A.D. 313 for his own selfish purposes to get political power. That's as ridiculous as saying that Communism wasn't invented until 1965, by Fidel Castro. All the data refute it. The belief that Jesus is divine is found in almost every single one of the thousands of books that were written by Christians between the death of Christ (ca. A.D. 30) and the time of Constantine (A.D. 313), starting with the twenty-seven books of the New Testament. Only historically ignorant and gullible people could believe such myths as The Da Vinci Code. — Peter J. Kreeft, *Because God Is Real: Sixteen Questions, One Answer* (San Francisco: Ignatius Press, 2008), 61–63.

8. The Bible is only words. Does God speak in words? Aren't feelings more important?

Words are the way we communicate with each other. So God used our language to communicate with us. If He had used anything else, like mystical experiences, it would have been private, not public; only a few people would "get it".

Of course feelings are important, but so are words. For feelings are expressed and communicated by words. (Feelings are also created by words, for instance—"I love you" or "I hate you.")

Words communicate facts as well as feelings. And if feelings aren't in line with facts, they can be destructive. A Chinese parable puts it this way: Fact, Faith, and Feeling are three people walking along a wall. As long as Faith keeps his eyes on Fact, all three keep walking. But when Faith takes his eyes off Fact and turns around to worry about how Feeling is doing, both Faith and Feeling fall off the wall, while Fact marches on. Our faith is not based on feelings but on facts.

Or, to change the image, feelings are like flowers, faith is like stems, and facts are like roots. The flowers are beautiful, but they are based on the stems, and the stems are based on the roots. This is true about our relationships to each other as well as our relationship with God. For instance, you feel affection toward your parents because you have faith that they love you, and you feel fear toward a screaming man running at you with a knife because you believe he wants to kill you. Those two beliefs, in turn, are based on objective facts. First fact, then faith, then feeling. — *Peter J. Kreeft, Because God Is Real: Sixteen Questions, One Answer (San Francisco: Ignatius Press, 2008), 67–69.*

9. **This week's interview is with Gary Collins. What is his expertise? What do you recall about him?**

    This topic is familiar territory to Witherington, whose books include The Christology of Jesus, Jesus the Sage, The Many Faces of the Christ, The Jesus Quest, Jesus, Paul, and the End of the World, Reading and Understanding the Bible, New Testament History, and commentaries on Mark, John, Acts, and Romans. His articles have been featured in specialized dictionaries and academic journals. — Lee Strobel, *The Case for Christ Movie Edition: Solving the Biggest Mystery of All Time* (Grand Rapids, MI: Zondervan, 2017).

10. **So far…**
    We have established that early writers recorded about Jesus…
    That this writing was faithfully transferred to us…
    That Jesus claimed to be God…
    But, maybe Jesus was crazy.
    Is anyone familiar with the famous C.S. Lewis poached egg quote? Do a search for "C.S. Lewis poached egg." What do you find?

    I am trying here to prevent anyone saying the really foolish things that people often say about Him: "I'm ready to accept Jesus as a great moral teacher, but I don't accept His claim to be God." That is the one thing we must not say. A man who was merely a man and said the sort of thing Jesus said would not be a great moral teacher. He would rather be a lunatic—on a level with the man who says he is a poached egg— Or else he would be the Devil of Hell. — Norman L. Geisler and Abdul Saleeb*, Answering Islam: The Crescent in Light of the Cross, 2nd ed*. (Grand Rapids, MI: Baker Books, 2002), 254.

11. So, here is this week's question: how do we know Jesus wasn't crazy… on the level of a man who says he is a poached egg?

Perhaps Jesus was crazy or possessed. Before we jump too quickly at this explanation, however, we need to ask whether the total character of Jesus (as we know it) bears out this speculation. Did he act like one who was crazy? Did he speak like one suffering from megalomania? It is hard to read the Gospels and be satisfied with this explanation. Rather, it is hard to escape the conclusion that Jesus was actually the sanest man who ever lived. He spoke with quiet authority. He always seemed in control of the situation. He was never surprised or rattled. He just does not seem to fit our easy classifications.

There is another reason why Jesus cannot have been crazy. It is the reaction of others to him. Men and women did not merely tolerate Jesus; they either were for him or else violently against him. This is not the way we react to those who are crazy. We may be irritated by a madman's irrational behavior. We may ignore him. We may lock him up if his delusions are dangerous. But we do not kill him. Yet this is what men who did not want to follow him tried to do to Jesus. — James Montgomery Boice, *The Gospel of John: An Expositional Commentary* (Grand Rapids, MI: Baker Books, 2005), 557.

12. There is actually one more possibility: perhaps Jesus was just mistaken. How would you respond to this view?

Dawkins insists, "There is no good historical evidence that [Jesus] ever thought he was divine." Regarding C. S. Lewis's explanation that in claiming to be the Son of God Jesus was either right, insane, or a liar, Dawkins offers "a fourth possibility, almost too obvious to need mentioning . . . that Jesus was honestly mistaken." Yet how can one be simply "mistaken" about thinking one is God? How could anyone think Jesus, who comes across as wise, humble, loving, truthful, and supremely self-sacrificing in the Scriptures, was insane, lying, or "honestly mistaken"?

C. S. Lewis regarded Jesus' teachings as the highest standard of morality known to man, and that creates a big problem for some, the problem of cosmic authority, according to Regis Nicoll: "If Jesus was right about his divinity, then man is not a morally autonomous happenstance, he's a special creation, a being that will one day stand before his Creator." Nicoll quotes one self-described atheist as saying, "It isn't just that I don't believe in God . . . I hope there is no God" (emphasis added). — Erwin Lutzer, *Seven Reasons Why You Can Trust the Bible* (Chicago, IL: Moody Publishers, 2008).

13. Mark 3.21. What did Jesus family think about his sanity or lack of?

Thinking Jesus was crazy, they sought to have him committed. No wonder Jesus later disclaims his mother and brothers when they come to see him. " 'Who are my mother and my brothers?' he asked. Then he looked at those seated in a circle around him and said, 'Here are my mother and my brothers! Whoever does God's will is my brother and sister and mother' " (Mark 3:32b–35). His brothers' lack of faith may explain why Jesus on the cross committed his mother to John's care, not to theirs (John 19:26–27). The memory of their unbelief may also be behind the refusal of James and Jude to call themselves brothers of Jesus in their letters, preferring the title "slave of Jesus Christ" (James 1:1; Jude 1). — Gary Holloway, James & Jude, *The College Press NIV Commentary* (Joplin, MO: College Press Pub., 1996), Jas.

14. Do you think they were seriously worried about Jesus being insane?

"Take charge" is actually "they went to seize him," using krateō, a verb often used in reference to arresting a criminal. They apparently want to force Jesus to return home with them and quit this foolish ministry. His mother may think that he is on the verge of a breakdown, but his brothers certainly think that he has gone crazy. — Grant R. Osborne, Mark, ed. Mark L. Strauss and John H. Walton, *Teach the Text Commentary Series* (Grand Rapids, MI: Baker Books, 2014), 60.

15. What caused Jesus' family to come around and believe in Him? What changed their mind?

Some who believed in Jesus after His death were skeptics during His life. Take Jesus' half-brother James. He didn't buy Jesus' claim to deity; in fact, James thought his older brother was nuts (Mark 3:21). But after the Resurrection, he became the leader of the Jerusalem church and was stoned to death for his belief that Jesus was God. Something extraordinary had happened. Paul tells us that James saw Jesus alive after He died (1 Corinthians 15:7). — Rick Cornish, *5 Minute Apologist: Maximum Truth in Minimum Time* (Colorado Springs, CO: NavPress, 2014).

16. Mark 3.30 suggests that some people thought he was demon possessed. You say?

The leaders from Jerusalem not only thought Jesus was crazy (3:21); they also accused Him of being demon-possessed (3:30). Jesus refuted their charges by a series of logical arguments. First, he stated that Satan casting out Satan would be self-destructive. Second, the expulsion of demons would be a defeat and not a victory for Satan. Third, such willful and deliberate refusal of the

Spirit's testimony was a sin that could never be forgiven. Such blasphemy of the Holy Spirit, which has become known as "the unpardonable sin," is attributing to Satan the works of the Holy Spirit demonstrated in Jesus' ministry. Having rejected the testimony of the Father, the Son, and now the Spirit's miraculous authentication, nothing more could be done for the salvation of those religious leaders. To come to such a conclusion about Jesus, after all of the evidence to the contrary, was unpardonable. If on the other hand, Jesus was strong enough to defeat Satan, then He could deal with sin and the devil (13:27–28) because He is the Savior and the Son of God. — Mark Bailey et al*., Nelson's New Testament Survey: Discover the Background, Theology and Meaning of Every Book in the New Testament* (Nashville: Word, 1999), 73–74.

17. What do we learn about following Jesus from this passage?

Jesus showed us that even when we work exclusively for the welfare of others, some may say we are evil. In the instance Mark describes, the Pharisees deliberately twisted the words and deeds of Jesus to make him appear evil.

The same thing happens to leaders today, even to those with the best motives and the highest standards. You will never be fairly judged at all times. It is possible to do nothing but good and still be attacked. Don't expect fairness in a fallen world.

Winston Churchill was perhaps the greatest leader of the twentieth century. His magnificent, courageous leadership of the British people during the darkest days of World War II inspired freedom-loving people everywhere. Yet in the first election after his leadership helped secure victory over the Nazis, he was immediately voted out of office! This is an example of what leaders often face. Universal appreciation doesn't always follow great leadership. — Bob Briner and Ray Pritchard, *The Leadership Lessons of Jesus* (Nashville: B&H, 1997).

18. Why did Jesus elicit such a negative reaction from people?

A few years ago one of the leading golfers on the professional tour was invited to play in a foursome with Gerald Ford, then president of the United States, Jack Nicklaus, and Billy Graham. The golfer was especially in awe of playing with Ford and Billy Graham (he had played frequently with Nicklaus before).

After the round of golf was finished, one of the other pros came up to the golfer and asked, "Hey, what was it like playing with the President and with Billy Graham?"

The pro unleashed a torrent of cursing, and in a disgusted manner said, "I don't need Billy Graham stuffing religion down my throat." With that he turned on his heel and stormed off, heading for the practice tee.

His friend followed the angry pro to the practice tee. The pro took out his driver and started to beat out balls in fury. His neck was crimson and it looked like steam was coming from his ears. His friend said nothing. He sat on a bench and watched. After a few minutes the anger of the pro was spent. He settled down. His friend said quietly, "Was Billy a little rough on you out there?" The pro heaved an embarrassed sigh and said, "No, he didn't even mention religion. I just had a bad round."

Astonishing. Billy Graham had said not a word about God, Jesus, or religion, yet the pro had stormed away after the game accusing Billy of trying to ram religion down his throat. How can we explain this? It's really not difficult. Billy Graham didn't have to say a word; he didn't have to give a single sideward glance to make the pro feel uncomfortable. Billy Graham is so identified with religion, so associated with the things of God, that his very presence is enough to smother the wicked man who flees when no man pursues. Luther was right, the pagan does tremble at the rustling of a leaf. He feels the hound of heaven breathing down his neck. He feels crowded by holiness even if it is only made present by an imperfect, partially sanctified human vessel.

The reaction of the golf pro to Billy Graham was similar to the reaction of Peter to Jesus Christ. "Depart from me, for I am a sinful man." Both felt the trauma of the presence of the Holy. Holiness provokes hatred. The greater the holiness, the greater the human hostility toward it. It seems insane. No man was ever more loving than Jesus Christ. Yet even his love provoked men to anger. His love was a perfect love, a transcendent and holy love, but His very love brought trauma to people. This kind of love is so majestic we can't stand it. — R. C. Sproul, *The Holiness of God* (Wheaton, IL: Tyndale House Publishers, 1993), 101–103.

19. From what you know of Jesus… did He act like a crazy man?

You're not an expert on how crazy people act. But a professor named Dr. Gary Collins can help. He has spent his career working with those who have mental disorders of all kinds. He offers us a list of some of the main signs of insanity. We can study his list, then take a good look at whether Jesus acted like a crazy person:

Symptom of Insanity	Action of Jesus
Unpredictable emotion; depression or anger at odd times	Jesus wept when his friend died and became angry when he saw people cheating the poor.
Imagining people are out to get you	Jesus did believe a friend was out to get him—and he was right.
Thinking problems; trouble carrying on long conversations.	Jesus' sermons were orderly and logical.

Does he sound crazy to you? Wouldn't you cry if one of your friends died? Or if you saw someone stealing from a poor person? Jesus kept things interesting—no doubt about that. But he never showed any of the classic signs of insanity. He reacted pretty normally in all of these situations. — Lee Strobel, *Case for Christ for Kids, Updated and Expanded* (Grand Rapids, MI: Zonderkidz, 2010).

20. Some have suggested that Jesus hypnotized people so that they thought they saw miracles. You say?

MAYBE HE WAS A GREAT HYPNOTIST. Perhaps you could hypnotize someone to think you were walking on water or controlling the weather. A good hypnotist could give you water and make you think you were drinking soda. Maybe that was how Jesus pulled off that trick where he seemed to change water into wine.

Let's compare Jesus' miracles to hypnotism:

Hypnotism	Miracles
Many people in an audience are resistant to hypnotism.	Jesus performed miracles in huge crowds.
People can usually be hypnotized only when they're willing.	Many of Jesus' enemies saw the miracles. They weren't willing at all!
Hypnotists need words. They can't hypnotize without speaking.	When Jesus changed water into wine, he never spoke to the people drinking it.

So, hypnotism doesn't really fit. There were simply too many witnesses. Jesus spoke to large, active crowds. That meant he had to speak up, instead of softly the way you hear hypnotists talk in movies. He didn't choose certain ideal subjects, but performed miracles everyone could see (including people who didn't want to see miracles at all). Sometimes he even performed miracles that happened miles away! (See John 4:43–54, for instance.) No one can hypnotize someone in the next town. — Lee Strobel, *Case for Christ for Kids, Updated and Expanded* (Grand Rapids, MI: Zonderkidz, 2010).

21. What do you want to recall from today's discussion?

22. How can we support one another in prayer this week?

Case for Christ / Lesson #9 / Chapter 9
Did Jesus Fulfill the Attributes of God?
Good Questions Have Groups Talking
www.joshhunt.com

DIG

1. **State your name and… If you could ask Lee Strobel one question, what would it be?**

2. **Who read Chapter 9 this week? What got your attention?**

3. **This week's lesson has to do with the deity of Christ. What did Jesus do to demonstrate His divinity?**

    Jesus' deity is clearly revealed not only by His divine names and attributes but also by His many miracles. The New Testament often refers to Jesus' miracles as signs (John 2:11). Signs always signify something—in this case, that Jesus is the divine Messiah.

    According to the New Testament, Jesus changed water into wine (John 2:7-8), healed the nobleman's son (John 4:50), healed Peter's mother-in-law (Matthew 8:15), caused the disciples to catch a great number of fish (Luke 5:5-6), healed a leper (Matthew 8:3), healed a paralytic (Matthew 9:2), healed a centurion's servant (Matthew 8:13), and raised a widow's son (Luke 7:14).

    He also calmed a stormy sea (Matthew 8:26), healed the Gadarene demoniac (Matthew 8:32), healed a woman with internal bleeding (Matthew 9:22), healed two blind men (Matthew 9:29), fed huge crowds with almost nothing (Matthew 14:19; 15:36), and walked on the sea (Matthew 14:25).

Still further, He healed a demoniac boy (Matthew 17:18; Mark 9:25; Luke 9:42), caused Peter to catch a fish with a coin in its mouth (Matthew 17:27), healed a woman with an 18-year infirmity (Luke 13:10-17), healed a man with dropsy (Luke 14:4), healed ten lepers (Luke 17:11-19), raised Lazarus from the dead (John 11:43-44), and restored (healed) a severed ear (Matthew 26:51). — Ron Rhodes, *5-Minute Apologetics for Today: 365 Quick Answers to Key Questions* (Eugene, OR: Harvest House, 2010).

4. Matthew 9.1, 2. How does this passage show Jesus' deity?

C. E. Jefferson states that "He forgave sins, He spoke as one having authority. Even the worst sinners when penitent at His feet received from Him authoritative assurance of forgiveness" (Jefferson, CJ, 330).

Lewis Sperry Chafer points out that "none on earth has either authority or right to forgive sin. None could forgive sin save the One against whom all have sinned. When Christ forgave sin, as He certainly did, He was not exercising a human prerogative. Since none but God can forgive sins, it is conclusively demonstrated that Christ, since He forgave sins, is God, and being God, is from everlasting" (Chafer, ST, vol. 5, 21). — Josh McDowell, *Evidence for Christianity* (Nashville, TN: Thomas Nelson Publishers, 2006), 363.

5. What is the application of this passage for our lives?

Christianity's most distinctive message is the truth that God can forgive sin. The essence of the gospel is that Christ's atoning death can free people from the penalty of sin. If Jesus can heal diseases and disabilities, He can surely provide cleansing for the consequences of sin. The men who brought the paralytic to the Lord undoubtedly believed this very strongly.

Those with crippling disabilities have always had to endure social stigma and neglect. But in the Jewish culture of Jesus' day and much earlier, the stigma was especially pronounced because everyone believed chronic ailments stemmed directly from someone's sin. Bildad told Job, "If your sons sinned against Him, then He delivered them into the power of their transgression" (Job 8:4; cf. 4:7; John 9:1–2).

The paralytic here likely had the same understanding concerning sin and disease, thus he was determined at any cost to see Jesus for forgiveness and a resultant physical healing. Christ saw the determination of his faith as his friends worked through the crowd to get the paralytic in front of Him. That aggressive approach revealed their hearts of faith. In all his physical ugliness and spiritual neediness, the man threw himself upon Jesus' mercy.

The paralyzed man came to the Lord in true humility and poverty of spirit, which God requires of all seeking hearts (Matt. 5:3). Jesus sometimes healed people of little faith, but He was especially willing to heal those of great faith, as with the men and his friends. — John MacArthur, *Daily Readings from the Life of Christ* (Chicago: Moody Publishers, 2008), 226.

6. **Philippians 2.5 – 9. Verse 7 says that Jesus emptied Himself (ESV). What did He empty Himself of? Did He empty Himself of His Deity?**

PROBLEM: Paul seems to say that Jesus "emptied Himself" of His deity or "equality with God" (vv. 6–7), becoming "a man" (v. 8). But elsewhere Jesus claimed to be God on earth (John 8:58; 20:28). But how could Jesus be God while on earth if He left His deity aside to become man?

SOLUTION: Jesus did not cease being God while on earth. Rather, in addition to being God, He also became man. His incarnation was not the subtraction of deity, but the addition of humanity. Several things in this text support this position. First, it does not say Christ gave up or emptied Himself of His deity, but merely of His rights as deity, assuming the "form of a servant" (v. 7) so as to be an example for us (v. 5). Second, the text declares that He was in the "form of God" or "in very nature God" (v. 6, NIV). Just as the "form of a servant" (v. 7) is a servant by nature, so the "form of God" (v. 6) is God by nature. Third, this very passage declares that every knee will one day confess Jesus is "Lord," a citation from Isaiah 45:23 that refers to Yahweh, a name used exclusively of God. — Norman L. Geisler and Thomas A. Howe, *When Critics Ask : A Popular Handbook on Bible Difficulties* (Wheaton, Ill.: Victor Books, 1992), 480.

7. Verse 6. What does this verse tell us about Jesus?

When Paul says that Christ Jesus was in the form of God, that is, in full possession of the divine nature, he underlines the fact by using, not the simple verb 'to be', but a stronger verb which in its characteristic usage has the force 'to be really and truly', 'to be characteristically', even 'to be by nature'. In a passage like the present one, where it is plain that every word has been weighed and measured, the full meaning of the verb can be assumed: he was really and truly, in his own personal and essential nature, God. — J. A. Motyer, *The Message of Philippians, The Bible Speaks Today* (Downers Grove, IL: InterVarsity Press, 1984), 112.

8. **Read for application. What does this tell us about what it means to be Christlike?**

Whereas verse 6 emphasized what the pre-incarnate Christ did not do, verse 7 indicates what He did do: He emptied himself. While the verb used here (kenoō) more commonly refers in Paul's writings to making something void, here it has the sense of 'divestiture of position or prestige.' In contrast to those who are motivated by conceit (kenodoxia) in 2:3, Christ emptied Himself (kenoō) to serve others. Throughout the centuries theologians have needlessly speculated what it means to say that the pre-incarnate Christ emptied Himself, leading some to conclude that Christ set aside certain divine attributes in becoming human. But the context itself explains what Christ's 'emptying Himself' means in the two clauses that follow, both of which describe the same action (the incarnation) from slightly different angles.28

First, Christ emptied Himself by taking the form of a servant. Whereas Christ was in the form (morphē) of God (2:6), here He takes on the form (morphēn) of a servant. The one who from all eternity existed as the radiant visible splendor of God concealed that glory by taking on the form of a servant. Just as saying that Christ was in the form of God indicated that His visible appearance truly expressed His true essence, so too saying that Christ took on the form of a servant means that His appearance as a servant matched His true essence. So to refer to Christ as taking 'the form of a servant' is the same as saying that He became a servant in the fullest sense of the word.

In saying that Christ took the form of a servant, Paul alludes to the Suffering Servant of Isaiah 52:13–53:12. Within the larger context of Isaiah 40–55, the nation of Israel is initially identified as the Servant of Yahweh, commissioned to be a light to the nations (Isa. 42:1–9). But Israel failed miserably in its mission (Isa. 42:18–25). Consequently God promises to raise up a new Servant who will obey where Israel failed, redeeming Israel and becoming a light for the nations (Isa. 49:1–7). He will accomplish this by willingly offering Himself as a substitutionary sacrifice for their sins and as a result will justify His people (Isa. 52:13–53:12). As a result of the Servant's work, the new covenant will be established (Isa. 54:1–17) and the offer of forgiveness through the Servant will be preached to the nations (Isa. 55:1–13). By saying that Christ took on the form of a servant, Paul is drawing upon that larger narrative to help us understand the work of Jesus Christ.

Second, Christ emptied Himself by being born in the likeness of men. Taking on the form of a servant required that Christ be born into this world as a man. By using the expression likeness of men Paul may be echoing the language of Genesis 1:26, where God says, 'Let us make man in our image, after our likeness.' If so, the point is that Christ was fully human in the same way that Adam and Eve were when they were originally created.35 Yet Paul also uses this same Greek word (homoiōma) in Romans 8:3, where he asserts that God sent Christ 'in the likeness of sinful flesh.' These passages bring together two key truths about the incarnate Christ— He was fully human, and yet He was without sin. — Matthew S. Harmon, *Philippians: A Mentor Commentary, Mentor Commentaries* (Great Britain; Ross-shire: Mentor, 2015), 210–212.

9. John 3.16. Who can quote this classic verse?

I am a little bit addicted to the Scripture Typer app. https://scripturetyper.com/

It is a based on sound educational theory:

- Memories are created when you struggle to remember. Just as muscles grow when you try to lift heavy weights, so memories grow when you put yourself in a situation where you struggle to recall.

- Memories are created through repeated and variegated exposure. By seeing, hearing, struggling, recalling, waiting a few days, and doing the whole process again, we memorize.

Scripture Typer is cross-platform. You can use it on your PC or mac. You can use it on your IPhone or IPad. You can use it on your android. You can use in on your Kindle Fire.

You start by typing the verse while looking at it. The browser version has you type the whole thing. The app version has you type the first letter of each word.

Once you have this down, you move to the second level. Now you can see every other word. By seeing every other word, you are forced to struggle a bit. It is in the struggling that memories are made.

Once you have it down, you type the whole thing without being able to see the verse. If you get it right, it goes into the review pile.

Tomorrow it will come up for review, and again the next day. If you get it right a few days in a row, ScriptureTyper will spread the reviews to every other day, then every third day and so forth. If you feel you need more review, you can reset it to review every day.

You can also record the verses you are working on and listen to them as you drive or exercise.

Of course, the real point is not to say that you can quote so many verses. The point is to use Scripture Memory as a means to meditation. The real point is to be transformed by the renewing of you mind. The real point is to strengthen you faith by hearing, learning, and meditating on God's Word.

If you are not in the habit of Scripture Memory, I highly recommend ScriptureTyper as an aid to Scripture Memory. It is the best thing that has happened to me spiritually in a long, long time. — Josh Hunt, *How to Live the Christian Life*, 2016.

10. Does this verse suggest that Jesus is not eternal? What exactly does "begotten" (KJV) mean?

What does the phrase "the only begotten Son of God" mean?

The term "only begotten" is used to describe the unique relationship between the Father and Jesus (John 1:14, 18; 3:16; 1 John 4:9). Though any individual who trusts Christ personally for salvation will become a child of God (John 1:12), there is only one "only begotten Son of God." In this phrase Christ possesses the nature of God, just as a son possesses the nature of his father. The only begotten Son of God is just like His heavenly Father, for He is God. — Elmer Towns, *Bible Answers for Almost All Your Questions* (Nashville: Thomas Nelson, 2003).

11. I don't want us to get too lost in the technical apologetics. What do we learn about ourselves from this verse? What is the application?

The heart of the human problem is the heart of the human. And God's treatment is prescribed in John 3:16.

He loves. He gave.

We believe. We live.

The words are to Scripture what the Mississippi River is to America—an entryway into the heartland. Believe or dismiss them, embrace or reject them, any serious consideration of Christ must include them. Would a British historian dismiss the Magna Carta? Egyptologists overlook the Rosetta stone? Could you ponder the words of Christ and never immerse yourself into John 3:16?

The verse is an alphabet of grace, a table of contents to the Christian hope, each word a safe-deposit box of jewels. Read it again, slowly and aloud, and note the word that snatches your attention. . . .

"God so loved the world . . ." We'd expect an anger-fueled God. One who punishes the world, recycles the world, forsakes the world . . . but loves the world?

The world? This world? Heartbreakers, hope snatchers, and dream dousers prowl this orb. Dictators rage. Abusers inflict. Reverends think they deserve the title. But God loves. And he loves the world so much he gave his: Declarations? Rules? Dicta? Edicts?

No. The heart-stilling, mind-bending, deal-making-or-breaking claim of John 3:16 is this: God gave his Son . . . his only Son. No abstract ideas, but a flesh-wrapped divinity. Scripture equates Jesus with God. God, then, gave himself. Why? So that "whoever believes in him shall not perish." —3:16: THE NUMBERS OF HOPE / Max Lucado, *Live Loved: Experiencing God's Presence in Everyday Life* (Nashville: Thomas Nelson, 2011).

12. What do we learn about God from this verse?

God gives. He is generous; He is lavishly generous.

That is God's way. He did it with his own Son, Jesus. He gave him away. He gave him to the nations. He did not keep him on display. He did not preserve him in a museum. He did not show him off as a trophy. "God so loved the world that he gave his only Son, so that everyone who believes in him may not perish but may have eternal life" (John 3:16, NRSV). — *RUN WITH THE HORSES* / Eugene H. Peterson, *God's Message for Each Day: Wisdom from the Word of God* (Nashville: Thomas Nelson, 2006).

13. Colossians 1.15. Does this suggest Jesus was created, not eternal?

What about Colossians 1:15–17? Jehovah's Witnesses refer to this passage to support their teaching that Christ was created by Jehovah (e.g., Let God Be True, p. 35). This is based primarily on the words "the firstborn of all creation" in verse 15.

However, if this verse were teaching that Jesus Christ is the first created being made by Jehovah, the word "first-created" would have been used of Christ, not the word "firstborn." These are two different words in the Greek, with two different meanings. "First-created" is protoktistos, and "firstborn" is prototokos.

Colossians 1:15 does not use the word protoktistos, "first-created." Instead it uses prototokos. This latter word means an heir, a begotten one, the first in rank. The teaching of Colossians 1:15, then, is that Christ is first in rank above all creation; He is the heir of all things. He is prior to all creation and superior over it as the Lord. — Roy B. Zuck, *An Open Letter to a Jehovah's Witness* (Chicago, IL: Moody Publishers, 2012).

14. We have friendly debates between members of many denominations. We disagree with them, but we see them as part of the family. Jehovah's Witnesses are not one of those groups. They are a cult. How do they (wrongly) interpret this passage?

Your New World Translation adds the word "other" four times in Colossians 1:15–17, so that the passage states that Christ created "all other things," that is, everything except Himself. However, there is no basis for adding the word "other." It does not occur in the Greek manuscripts. The translators of the New World Translation admit this by putting the word "other" in brackets. Obviously this is done in order to comply with the assumption that firstborn means first-created. But, as we've seen, this is not the meaning of firstborn, and therefore it is also wrong to add the word "other." There is no verse in the entire Bible that states that Christ was created by Jehovah!

Some might raise a question about Revelation 3:14. This passage, wrongly translated in the New World Translation "the beginning of the creation of God," should be rendered "the source [or origin] of God's creation." The Greek word for source or origin is archiē. This is consistent with the statement in Colossians 1:16 and John 1:3 that all things were made by or had their origin in Jesus Christ. Since all things were made by Christ (John 1:1) and all things were made by Jehovah (Hebrews 3:4), both persons possessing this omnipotent creative power are God with full deity. — Roy B. Zuck, *An Open Letter to a Jehovah's Witness* (Chicago, IL: Moody Publishers, 2012).

15. **Let's close by looking at four verses in rapid fire succession. With each, we want to ask the same question. How does this verse show the deity of Christ? First, John 16.30.**

Jesus Christ is described as an eternal (Micah 5:2; John 1:1; Col. 1:17), omnipotent (Rev. 19:16), omniscient (Matt. 11:27; John 2:24–25; 16:30), omnipresent (Matt. 18:20), Holy (John 6:69), immutable (Heb. 1:10–12; 13:8), and true deity (1 John 5:20). No mere creature could be described as such without committing blasphemy. — Robert A. Morey, *The Trinity: Evidence and Issues* (Iowa Falls, IA: World Pub., 1996), 373.

16. **Matthew 28.20 and Matthew 18.20. How does these verses show the deity of Christ?**

When Christ said to His disciples, "I have been given complete authority in heaven and on earth," the promise immediately followed, "I am with you always" (Matthew 28:18, 20). The Omnipotent One is truly the Omnipresent One. The writer of Psalm 139 speaks of God's omnipresence as something beyond his comprehension: "Such knowledge is too wonderful for me, too great for me to know!" (verse 6).

The revelation of God's omnipresence in the man Christ Jesus makes the mystery still deeper. The fact that we can experience this presence every moment is inexpressibly wonderful. And yet many of us find it difficult to understand all that Christ's presence implies and how, through prayer, it can become the practical experience of our daily life.

When Christ says "always," He means to give us the assurance that there should never be a moment in which that presence cannot be our experience. Yet, it does not depend upon what we can effect, but upon what He undertakes to do.

The omnipotent Christ is indeed the omnipresent Christ. His promise to us is: "I am with you always." Let your faith in Christ, the Omnipresent One, be in the quiet confidence that He will be with you every day and every moment. Meet Him in prayer, and let His presence be your strength for service. — Andrew Murray, *Teach Me to Pray: Lightly-Updated Devotional Readings from the Works of Andrew Murray* (Uhrichsville, OH: Barbour, 2012).

17. Matthew 28.18. How does this verse show the deity of Christ?

All power is given—unto whom? To the Being who lived a humble, obscure life in Nazareth; the One who says "Come unto Me, all ye that labour and are heavy laden, and I will give you rest." If all power is given to Jesus Christ, what right have I to insult Him by worrying? If we will let these words of Jesus come into our heart, we shall soon see how contemptible our unbelief is. Jesus Christ will do anything for us in keeping with His own character; the power that comes from Him is stamped with His nature. Will I say sceptically, "What does Jesus Christ know about my circumstances? Is His power and understanding sufficient to manage things for me?" To talk like that is the way to realise the size of our unbelief, and to see why Jesus Christ was so stern in condemning it.

"All power is given unto Me," and yet Paul says "He was crucified through weakness," and, he adds, "we also are weak in Him." Am I powerful enough to be weak? Any weak man can strike another back, it takes a strong man to take it meekly; the omnipotence of Jesus at work in a man means that neither the world, the flesh or the

devil can make him show anything but Christ-likeness.
— Oswald Chambers, *Bringing Sons into Glory: Studies in the Life of Our Lord* (London: Marshall, Morgan & Scott, 1996).

18. John 1.1. How does this verse show the deity of Christ?

Jesus Christ, God incarnate, also verified His deity and His eternality to the people of His day by declaring to them, "Before Abraham was born, I AM" (John 8:58). It is clear that Jesus was claiming to be God in flesh because the Jews, upon hearing this statement, tried to stone Him to death. To the Jews, declaring oneself to be the eternal God was blasphemy worthy of death (Leviticus 24:16). Jesus was claiming to be eternal, just as His Father is eternal. This was declared again by John regarding the nature of Christ: "In the beginning was the Word, and the Word was with God, and the Word was God" (John 1:1). From before recorded time, Jesus and His Father were one in essence, and sharing equally in the attribute of eternality. — Got Questions Ministries, *Got Questions? Bible Questions Answered* (Bellingham, WA: Logos Bible Software, 2002–2013).

19. Hebrews 13.8. How does this verse show the deity of Christ?

God is the same; goodness is as amiable in his sight, and sin as abominable in his eyes now, as it was at the beginning of the world. Being the same God, he is the same enemy to the wicked, as the same friend to the righteous; he is the same in knowledge, and cannot forget sinful acts; he is the same in will, and cannot approve of unrighteous practices; goodness cannot but be always the object of his love, and wickedness cannot but be always the object of his hatred; and as his aversion to sin is always the same, so as he has been in his judgments upon sinners, the same he will be still; for the same perfection of immutability belongs to his justice for the punishment of sin, as to his holiness for his disaffection to sin. — STEPHEN CHARNOCK / Elliot Ritzema and Elizabeth Vince, eds., *300 Quotations for Preachers from the Puritans, Pastorum Series* (Bellingham, WA: Lexham Press, 2013).

20. What do you want to recall from today's discussion?

21. How can we support one another in prayer this week?

Case for Christ / Lesson #10 / Chapter 10
Did Jesus and Jesus Alone Match the Identity of the Messiah?
Good Questions Have Groups Talking
www.joshhunt.com

DIG

1. **Who read Chapter 10 this week? What got your attention?**

2. **What are some Old Testament prophecies the point to Christ?**

Born in Bethlehem	Micah 5:2
Born a virgin	Isaiah 7:14
A Prophet like Moses	Deut. 18:15, 18–19
Entered Jerusalem in Triumph	Zech. 9:9
Rejected by His own	Isaiah 53:1, 3; Psalm 118:22
Betrayed by one of His own followers	Psalm 41:9
Tried and condemned	Isaiah 53:8
Silent before His accusers	Isaiah 53:7
Struck and spat on by enemies	Isaiah 50:6
Mocked and insulted	Psalm 22:7–8
Die by crucifixion	Psalm 22:14, 16–17
Suffer with criminals and pray for his enemies	Isaiah 53:12

Given vinegar	Psalm 69:21
Others to cast lots for His Garments	Psalm 22:18
His bones were not to be broken	Exodus 12:46
To die as a sacrifice for sin	Isaiah 53:5–6, 8
Raised from the dead	Psalm 16:10
Now at God's right hand	Psalm 110:1

Johnston M. Cheney, Stanley A. Ellisen, and Johnston M. Cheney, *Jesus Christ The Greatest Life: A Unique Blending of the Four Gospels* (Eugene, OR: Paradise Publishing Inc., 1999), 13.

3. **Isaiah 53:2 – 10. Background. Roughly when was this written? If you have a Study Bible, you might look for notes on the introduction to Isaiah.**

Isaiah ("Yahweh saves") is said to be the son of Amoz, but we do not have any information about Amoz or any other of Isaiah's family. Information about the book's date and location is by implication. All of Isaiah's activity seems to have been in and around Jerusalem, and his messages were apparently delivered between the dates of King Uzziah's death (739 BC) and Sennacherib's attack on Judah (701 BC). The book itself mentions only one author: "Isaiah son of Amoz" (1:1; 2:1; 13:1). — D. A. Carson, ed., *NIV Zondervan Study Bible: Built on the Truth of Scripture and Centered on the Gospel Message* (Grand Rapids, MI: Zondervan, 2015), 1307.

4. **What do we learn about this passage written 700 years before Jesus' birth?**

1. The Servant has humble origins with little outward prospects for success (53:1–2).

2. He experiences suffering and affliction (53:3).

3. The Servant accepts vicarious and substitutionary suffering on behalf of his people (53:4–6, 12).

4. He is put to death after being condemned (53:7–9).

5. Incredibly, he comes back to life and is exalted above all rulers (53:10–12; 52:13–15).

In addition to Helyer's observations, we note that the servant is also sinless (53:9). — Norman L. Geisler and Frank Turek, *I Don't Have Enough Faith to Be an Atheist* (Wheaton, IL: Crossway Books, 2004), 333.

5. How do we know this wasn't written after Christ?

In March of 1947 a young Arab shepherd boy (Muhammad adh-Dhib) was watching his sheep seven-and-a-half miles south of Jericho and one mile west of the Dead Sea. After tossing a rock at a stray goat, he heard the sound of breaking pottery. What ensued was one of the greatest archaeological discoveries of all time—the Dead Sea Scrolls.

In excavations of area caves through 1956, numerous scrolls and thousands of manuscript fragments were found in pottery that had been placed there about 2,000 years ago by a Jewish religious sect known as the Essenes. The Essenes existed as a group from 167 B.C. to A.D. 68. They had broken away from the temple authorities and established their own monastic community in the Judean desert near Qumran.

One of their scrolls found in Qumran is now known as the Great Isaiah Scroll. Dated from 100 B.C., this twenty-four-foot scroll is the complete book of Isaiah (all sixty-six chapters) and is the oldest biblical scroll in existence. It is currently protected in a vault somewhere in Jerusalem, but a copy of it is on display at the Shrine of the Book museum in Jerusalem.

The importance of this discovery is not just that the scroll predates Christ and is in good condition, but that it contains perhaps the clearest and most complete prophecy about the coming Messiah. Isaiah calls the Messiah the "Servant of the Lord," and he begins to refer to the Servant in chapter 42 in what is known as the first "Servant Song." However, the Servant is most often referred to as the "Suffering Servant," because of the vivid description of his sacrificial death found in Isaiah 53. — Norman L. Geisler and Frank Turek, *I Don't Have Enough Faith to Be an Atheist* (Wheaton, IL: Crossway Books, 2004), 329–330.

6. How do Jews who don't believe in Christ see this passage?

Further confirmation of the predictive nature of Isaiah 53 is that it was common for Jewish interpreters before the time of Christ to teach that here Isaiah spoke of the Jewish Messiah (see S. R. Driver et al., trans., The Fifty-Third Chapter of Isaiah According to Jewish Interpreters). Only after early Christians began using the text apologetically with great force did it become in rabbinical teaching an expression of the suffering Jewish nation. Yet this view is implausible in the context of Isaiah's standard references to the Jewish people in the first-person plural ("our" or "we"), whereas he always refers to the Messiah in the third-person singular, as in Isaiah 53 ("he" and "his" and "him") (Geisler, BECA, 612). — Josh McDowell, *Evidence for Christianity* (Nashville, TN: Thomas Nelson Publishers, 2006), 223–224.

7. Some Jews see this as a picture of Israel. What is wrong with this picture?

Unfortunately for Rashi and many present-day Jewish theologians, there are at least three fatal flaws with the assertion that Israel is the Suffering Servant. First, unlike Israel, the Servant is sinless (53:9). To say that Israel is sinless is to contradict and negate virtually the entire Old Testament. The recurrent theme of the Old Testament is that Israel has sinned by breaking God's commandments and by chasing after other gods instead of the one true God. If Israel is sinless, then why did God give the Jews a sacrificial system? Why did they have a Day of Atonement? Why did they constantly need prophets to warn them to stop sinning and to come back to God?

Second, unlike Israel, the Suffering Servant is a lamb who submits without any resistance whatsoever (53:7). History shows us that Israel certainly is not a lamb—she lies down for no one.

Third, unlike Israel, the Suffering Servant dies as a substitutionary atonement for the sins of others (53:4–6, 8, 10–12). But Israel has not died, nor is she paying for the sins of others. No one is redeemed on account of what the nation of Israel does. Nations, and the individuals that comprise them, are punished for their own sins.

This Johnny-come-lately interpretation of Isaiah 53 appears to be motivated by the desire to avoid the conclusion that Jesus is indeed the Messiah who was predicted hundreds of years beforehand. But there's no legitimate way to avoid the obvious. Remember, the Great Isaiah Scroll was written some 100 years before Christ, and we know that the material it contains is even older. The Septuagint, which is the translation of the Hebrew Old Testament (including all of Isaiah) into

Greek, is dated about 250 B.C. So the Hebrew original must be even older. Furthermore, manuscripts or manuscript fragments of all the Old Testament books except Esther were found with the Dead Sea Scrolls. So there's no doubt that the Old Testament, including the Suffering Servant passage, predates Christ by several hundred years. — Norman L. Geisler and Frank Turek, *I Don't Have Enough Faith to Be an Atheist* (Wheaton, IL: Crossway Books, 2004), 333–334.

8. Why can't Jews see Jesus in this passage?

To whom do you think this is referring? Barry had a good idea who. Reading out of his own Tanach, he was startled at the parallels to Jesus, but he was still a bit confused. He wanted to give his rabbi a chance to explain it.

"I vividly remember the first time I seriously confronted Isaiah 53, or better still, the first time it seriously confronted me," Barry explains. "Being rather confused over the identity of the Servant in Isaiah 53, I went to my local rabbi and said to him, 'Rabbi, I have met some people at school who claim that the so-called Servant in Isaiah 53 is none other than Jesus of Nazareth. But I would like to know from you, who is this Servant in Isaiah 53?' "

Barry was astonished at his response. The rabbi said, "Barry, I must admit that as I read Isaiah 53 it does seem to be talking about Jesus, but since we Jews do not believe in Jesus, it can't be speaking about Jesus."

Barry didn't know a lot about formal logic at that point, but he knew enough to say to himself, "That just doesn't sound kosher to me! Not only does the rabbi's so-called reasoning sound circular, it also sounds evasive and even fearful." Today Barry observes, "There are none who are as deaf as those who do not want to hear." — Norman L. Geisler and Frank Turek, *I Don't Have Enough Faith to Be an Atheist* (Wheaton, IL: Crossway Books, 2004), 332.

9. Isaiah 53.2. Tender shoot. What is that talking about?

Here is the report of the One who is coming. First, He is the sensitive One. So tenderhearted is Jesus that, even as He was dying on the cross, He looked down and saw His mother with John. In the midst of unbelievable suffering He said to her, "Behold thy son," and to John, "behold thy mother" (John 19:26, 27), making sure that His mother would be cared for after His death. — Jon Courson, *Jon Courson's Application Commentary: Volume Two: Psalms-Malachi* (Nashville, TN: Thomas Nelson, 2006), 445.

10. What is meant by the dry ground in this same verse?

When Jesus came on the scene, the ground was dry indeed. Politically, Rome had been oppressing the people of Israel. Spiritually, the people had received no word from God, no miracles, no prophecies for four hundred years.

In Jeremiah 2, the Lord said, "My people have committed two evils. They have forsaken Me, the fountain of living water, and they have carved out cisterns that can hold no water." If you're dry because you've forsaken the living water to draw from the cistern of occupational success, materialistic pursuits, or even family or friend relationships, you'll eventually find that it doesn't hold water, that it's a broken cistern. It won't refresh you the way you thought it would.

"If any man thirst, let him come unto Me and drink," Jesus says. "And out of his innermost being shall gush forth torrents of living water" (see John 7:37, 38). If you're in a dry place, consider the sensitive One, Jesus Christ, who comes in dry times to those who thirst for more. — Jon Courson, *Jon Courson's Application Commentary: Volume Two: Psalms-Malachi* (Nashville, TN: Thomas Nelson, 2006), 445.

11. Verse 4, 5. Circle every occurrence of the word "our." What do we learn about ourselves from these two verses?

An artist by the name of Steinberg once asked an uneducated gypsy girl to sit for him. At the time he was working on another painting, Christ on the Cross, and the girl saw him working on it. She observed about Christ, 'He must have been a very wicked man to be nailed to a cross like that.' Steinberg quickly corrected her: 'No, on the contrary, he was a very good man, the best man that ever lived. He died for others.' That is what Isaiah is saying here, four times in two verses: '... our griefs ... our sorrows ... our transgressions ... our iniquities' (53:4–5, emphasis added). The Servant is not being punished for anything he has done; he is there in the place of others. He is a substitute. The gypsy girl's response to Steinberg's explanation that the man on the cross had died for others was to ask him a question: 'Did he die for you?' It unsettled Steinberg, because he didn't feel comfortable answering yes. It is said that he carried on thinking about it until he knew in this heart, and could say with confidence, that Jesus had died for him. — Andrew Thomson, *Opening Up Isaiah, Opening Up Commentary* (Leominster: Day One, 2012), 133.

12. Verse 6. What does this verse reveal about Jesus?

Jesus is the sin-bearing One. In 1 John 2:2, we read that Jesus died not only for our sins but for the sins of the whole world. What a shock that must have been. Here, One who had never sinned, who knew nothing of sin, suddenly took on all of the sin ever committed by everyone who has ever lived. The best estimates are that there are seventy-seven billion people who have lived on this planet. And Jesus absorbed all of their sin—except the blasphemy of the Spirit, which is a person's rejection of Him. "For he hath made him to be sin for us, who knew no sin ; that we might be made the righteousness of God in him" (2 Corinthians 5:21). Amazing grace. — Jon Courson, *Jon Courson's Application Commentary: Volume Two: Psalms-Malachi* (Nashville, TN: Thomas Nelson, 2006), 446.

13. What does this passage tell us about ourselves?

Isaiah writes as if we were there at the cross, because we were. If it wasn't our guilt that required the death of Jesus, what did? Remember Rembrandt's painting, "The Raising of the Cross," how he paints himself into the picture as one of the men crucifying the Lord? He not only portrays Jesus; he includes himself in the scene. Isaiah is doing that here, not with a brush on canvas but with a pen on paper. He's not only describing Jesus; he's telling our story too. We cannot say, "If I had been there, I wouldn't have shouted 'Crucify him!' "

Isaiah brings us to the heart of his message. Do you see what he's saying? Jesus really was a man of sorrows, but they weren't his own. He didn't deserve them. They were our sorrows. In a way we don't understand, Jesus substituted himself for us at the cross. God has done what we'd have no right to do—God has shifted the blame to Jesus Christ as he died for guilty people.

God has pointed the finger. He has laid on him the iniquity of us all. — Raymond C. Ortlund Jr. and R. Kent Hughes, *Isaiah: God Saves Sinners, Preaching the Word* (Wheaton, IL: Crossway Books, 2005), 356–357.

14. How does the passage inform our understanding of the cross?

Theologians call this imputation, from the Latin verb imputare, "to charge (to someone's account)." Guilt must be paid for. It can't be swept under the rug. You know that from your own experience. When you are wronged or injured—even in a fender-bender— someone has to answer for it, either you or the other person. The damage and cost don't just go away. If it's going to be put right, someone has to pay the cost. And so it is with God. There is no way he can turn a blind eye to our evil that is damaging his universe. How did God confront it? How was the damage paid for? Out of love for us, God charged that infinite debt to a substitute. Jesus Christ put himself in the place of sinners, the unbearable weight of their guilt was imputed to him, and he sank under it. "God made him who had no sin to be sin for us, so that in him we might become the righteousness of God" (2 Corinthians 5:21, NIV). This is the love of God.

Substitution is the very meaning of love. In A Tale of Two Cities, Sydney Carton takes another man's place at the guillotine and defeats Madame Defarge's lust for revenge. As he's about to die, a young girl also to be executed realizes that Carton has changed places with the condemned man. She tells him, "I think you were sent to me by Heaven." Dying love, real love, comes from God. Our part is to recognize in Jesus the only true love that exists and say to him, "I think you were sent to me by Heaven." — Raymond C. Ortlund Jr. and R. Kent

Hughes, *Isaiah: God Saves Sinners, Preaching the Word* (Wheaton, IL: Crossway Books, 2005), 357.

15. Verse 7. He did not open His mouth. What is the point?

Verse 7 compares Jesus to a lamb led to slaughter and a sheep silent before its shearers. What's the point? His death was not a capitulation to weakness but an exercise of deliberate control. He was not overpowered. He chose not to fight back. "He stood up in humble service for the sick and wicked, without questions or objections. He received what came, from man or God, without any protest whatsoever." — Raymond C. Ortlund Jr. and R. Kent Hughes, *Isaiah: God Saves Sinners, Preaching the Word* (Wheaton, IL: Crossway Books, 2005), 358.

16. Read for application. What is the application of this passage? What are we to do? How are we to respond?

Look at him. By faith look at him hanging there on his cross. What is he saying to you by his sacrifice? "Come to me, all who labor and are heavy laden, and I will give you rest" (Matthew 11:28). "Come, for everything is now ready" (Luke 14:17). "Come to me … and I will make with you an everlasting covenant" (Isaiah 55:3). Look at him. By faith, see his dying love for you. What is it worth? His blood is flowing down into pools at the foot of that cross. But it doesn't lie there in waste and loss. It flows out toward us—guilty, sad us. His blood flows out toward a woman who has shamed herself in a desperate craving to be loved. His blood washes her shame clean off her. Then that shame flows back to the cross, where it shames Jesus and is no longer her burden to bear. His blood flows out toward a man held in bondage to lust. He has discovered too late that there is no comfort there, only emptiness and self-hatred. But the blood of

Jesus flows out to that man, cleanses him entirely, and takes that painful wrong back to the cross where Jesus suffers for it as his own wrong, freeing that man forever.

The blood of Jesus is flowing out to sinners of all kinds, taking from them their guilt, their shame, their loss, their tears and despair, and giving them a whole new life. Jesus is saying to you right now, "I don't want you to bear your burden one moment longer. Let my chastisement give you peace. Let my stripes heal you." We are all like stupid sheep, wandering off from him through our own futile self-remedies and self-righteous excuses. Who can deny it? But look what God has done. God has laid on Christ the iniquity of us all. Believe it, and entrust your guilt to him. He can't bear it and survive, but he's still willing to bear it. — Raymond C. Ortlund Jr. and R. Kent Hughes, *Isaiah: God Saves Sinners, Preaching the Word* (Wheaton, IL: Crossway Books, 2005), 357–358.

17. Do you see the plan of Salvation in this 2700-year-old passage? How so?

This Servant is the substitute we all need, because we have all 'gone astray' (53:6). The following story is told about D. L. Moody, the nineteenth-century American evangelist, after he had been speaking at a mission service. He was hurrying away to catch a train when a man from the meeting caught up with him to ask for help, having realized that he needed to be saved. Moody was in danger of missing his train so he kept his words to a minimum: 'Look up Isaiah 53:6. Go in at the first "all" and go out at the last "all". Good night.' The man went home to see if he could work out what Moody was talking about. He saw the first 'all'—'All we like sheep have gone astray'—and readily accepted that he was included in that. Then he saw that he could also be included in the last 'all' — 'the Lord has laid on him the iniquity of us all'; his iniquities could be laid on Christ. That is what enables someone to say with confidence, 'Yes, Christ died for me.' — Andrew Thomson, *Opening Up Isaiah, Opening Up Commentary* (Leominster: Day One, 2012), 133–134.

18. What does Psalm 16.10 predict about Christ?

as the "Suffering Servant" prophecy, also details the death of Messiah for the sins of His people. More than 700 years before Jesus was even born, Isaiah provides details of His life and death. The Messiah will be rejected (Isaiah 53:3; Luke 13:34). The Messiah will be killed as a vicarious sacrifice for the sins of His people (Isaiah 53:5–9; 2 Corinthians 5:21). The Messiah will be silent in front of His accusers (Isaiah 53:7; 1 Peter 2:23). The Messiah will be buried with the rich (Isaiah 53:9; Matthew 27:57–60). The Messiah will be with criminals in His death (Isaiah 53:12; Mark 15:27).

In addition to the death of the Jewish Messiah, His resurrection from the dead is also foretold. The clearest and best known of the resurrection prophecies is the one penned by Israel's King David in Psalm 16:10, also written a millennium before the birth of Jesus: "For You will not abandon my soul to Sheol; Nor will You allow Your Holy One to undergo decay."

On the Jewish feast day of Shavuot (Weeks or Pentecost), when Peter preached the first gospel sermon, he boldly asserted that God had raised Jesus the Jewish Messiah from the dead (Acts 2:24). He then explained that God had performed this miraculous deed in fulfillment of David's prophecy in Psalm 16. In fact, Peter quoted the words of David in detail as contained in Psalm 16:8–11. Some years later, Paul did the same thing when he spoke to the Jewish community in Antioch.

Like Peter, Paul declared that God had raised Messiah Jesus from the dead in fulfillment of Psalm 16:10 (Acts 13:33–35). — *Got Questions Ministries, Got Questions? Bible Questions Answered* (Bellingham, WA: Logos Bible Software, 2002–2013).

19. What do you want to recall from today's study?

20. How can we support one another in prayer this week?

Case for Christ / Lesson #11 / Chapter 11
Was Jesus' Death a Sham and His Resurrection a Hoax?
Good Questions Have Groups Talking
www.joshhunt.com

DIG

1. **Who read Chapter 11 this week? What got your attention?**

2. **Do a Google search for: "Srinagar, Kashmir Jesus tomb" (no quotes). What do you find?**

   In addition to the major Muslim sects, there are several minor ones. The Wahhabis, who are primarily in Saudi Arabia, a strong legalistic group who are a radical wing of the Sunnis. Osama bin Laden was a Wahhabi. The Druze sect is located primarily in Lebanon, Syria, and northern Palestine. The Alawite sect is mostly in Syria. The Ahmadiyas are a heretical Muslim group from Pakistan whose founder, Mirza Ghulam Ahmad, claimed to be the promised Mahdi and Messiah. They also believe that Jesus, after escaping crucifixion, went to Kashmir and died in Srinagar. They also deny the virgin birth and sinless nature of Christ, discrediting any superiority of Christ over Muhammad. They are the most active Muslim missionary group in the West. — Norman L. Geisler and Abdul Saleeb, *Answering Islam: The Crescent in Light of the Cross, 2nd ed.* (Grand Rapids, MI: Baker Books, 2002), 299.

3. **They call this the swoon theory. What is meant by the swoon theory?**

   This theory implies that Jesus was not really dead, and that after a temporary loss of consciousness He revived and appeared to His disciples. — Conrad Emil Lindberg, *Apologetics or A System of Christian Evidence, Lutheran Seminary Text Book Series* (Rock Island, IL: Augustana Book Concern, 1917), 122.

4. **Overview. We are going to get into the detail, but, before we do, how would you respond to the swoon theory?**

   Nine pieces of evidence refute the swoon theory:

   1. Jesus could not have survived crucifixion. Roman procedures were very careful to eliminate that possibility. Roman law even laid the death penalty on any soldier who let a capital prisoner escape in any way, including bungling a crucifixion. It was never done.

   2. The fact that the Roman soldier did not break Jesus' legs, as he did to the other two crucified criminals (Jn 19:31–33), means that the soldier was sure Jesus was dead. Breaking the legs hastened the death so that the corpse could be taken down before the sabbath (v. 31).

   3. John, an eyewitness, certified that he saw blood and water come from Jesus' pierced heart (Jn 19:34–35). This shows that Jesus' lungs had collapsed and he had died of asphyxiation. Any medical expert can vouch for this.

   4. The body was totally encased in winding sheets and entombed (Jn 19:38–42).

   5. The postresurrection appearances convinced the disciples, even "doubting Thomas," that Jesus was

gloriously alive (Jn 20:19–29). It is psychologically impossible for the disciples to have been so transformed and confident if Jesus had merely struggled out of a swoon, badly in need of a doctor. A half-dead, staggering sick man who has just had a narrow escape is not worshiped fearlessly as divine lord and conqueror of death.

6. How were the Roman guards at the tomb overpowered by a swooning corpse? Or by unarmed disciples? And if the disciples did it, they knowingly lied when they wrote the Gospels, and we are into the conspiracy theory, which we will refute shortly.

7. How could a swooning half-dead man have moved the great stone at the door of the tomb? Who moved the stone if not an angel? No one has ever answered that question. Neither the Jews nor the Romans would move it, for it was in both their interests to keep the tomb sealed; the Jews had the stone put there in the first place, and the Roman guards would be killed if they let the body "escape."

The story the Jewish authorities spread, that the guards fell asleep and the disciples stole the body (Mt 28:11–15), is unbelievable. Roman guards would not fall asleep on a job like that; if they did, they would lose their lives. And even if they did fall asleep, the crowd and the effort and the noise it would have taken to move an enormous boulder would have wakened them. Furthermore, we are again into the conspiracy theory, with all its unanswerable difficulties (see next section).

8. If Jesus awoke from a swoon, where did he go? Think this through: you have a living body to deal with now, not a dead one. Why did it disappear? There is absolutely no data, not even any false, fantastic, imagined data, about Jesus' life after his crucifixion,

in any sources, friend or foe, at any time, early or late. A man like that, with a past like that, would have left traces.

9. Most simply, the swoon theory necessarily turns into the conspiracy theory or the hallucination theory, for the disciples testified that Jesus did not swoon but really died and really rose.

It may seem that these nine arguments have violated our initial principle about not presupposing the truth of the Gospel texts, since we have argued from data in the texts. But the swoon theory does not challenge the truths in the texts which we refer to as data; it uses them and explains them (by swoon rather than resurrection). Thus we use them too. We argue from our opponents' own premises. — Peter Kreeft and Ronald K. Tacelli, *Handbook of Christian Apologetics: Hundreds of Answers to Crucial Questions* (Downers Grove, IL: InterVarsity Press, 1994), 183–184.

5. **Let's walk through the last 18 hours of Jesus earthly life. First, let's turn to Luke 22.44. Jesus sweat drops of blood. What is that about?**

The night before Jesus Christ was crucified, He prayed in the garden of Gethsemane. It is in Luke's gospel where we see that His sweat was like drops of blood: "And being in agony, He prayed more earnestly. Then His sweat became like great drops of blood falling down to the ground" (Luke 22:44). "Hematidrosis" is a rare, but very real, medical condition where one's sweat will contain blood. The sweat glands are surrounded by tiny blood vessels. These vessels can constrict and then dilate to the point of rupture where the blood will then effuse into the sweat glands. It's cause—extreme anguish. In the other Gospel accounts, we see Jesus' level of anguish: "My soul is overwhelmed with sorrow to the point of death" (Matthew 26:38; Mark 14:34).

The intense anguish and sorrow Jesus felt was certainly understandable. Being God, Christ knew "all that was going to happen to Him" (John 18:4). He knew in painstaking detail the events that were to follow soon after He was betrayed by one of His very own disciples. Although our Savior never lied (1 Peter 2:22; Isaiah 53:9), He knew was about to undergo several trials where all of the witnesses against Him would do nothing but lie. He knew that many who hailed Him as the Messiah only days earlier would now be screaming for His crucifixion (Luke 23:23). He knew He would be flogged nearly to the point of death before they pounded the metal spikes into His flesh. He knew the prophetic words of Isaiah spoken seven centuries earlier that He would be beaten so badly that He would be "disfigured beyond that of any man" and "beyond human likeness" (Isaiah 52:14). Certainly these things factored into His great anguish and sorrow, causing Him to sweat drops of blood. — *Got Questions Ministries, Got Questions? Bible Questions Answered* (Bellingham, WA: Logos Bible Software, 2002–2013).

6. What would cause Jesus to sweat drops of blood?

Another historically accurate detail can be found in Luke 22:44. That's where Luke records that Jesus was in agony and sweat drops of blood the night before his crucifixion. Apparently, Jesus was experiencing a rare stress-induced condition we know today as hematohidrosis. That's when tiny blood vessels rupture due to extreme stress, thus allowing blood to mix with sweat. Since Luke probably didn't know of this medical condition 2,000 years ago, he could not have recorded it unless he had access to someone who saw it.

Details like this led William Ramsay (mentioned above) to say, "Luke's history is unsurpassed in respect of its trustworthiness," and "Luke is an historian of the first rank.... [He] should be placed along with the very greatest of historians." The bottom line is that Luke can be trusted. Since he has been confirmed independently on so many testable points, there's every reason to believe he's telling the truth elsewhere. — Norman L. Geisler and Frank Turek, *I Don't Have Enough Faith to Be an Atheist* (Wheaton, IL: Crossway Books, 2004), 262.

7. **Luke 19.1 says that Jesus was flogged. What was that flogging like?**

The Roman flogging or scourging that Jesus endured prior to being crucified normally consisted of 39 lashes, but could have been more (Mark 15:15; John 19:1). The whip that was used, called a flagrum, consisted of braided leather thongs with metal balls and pieces of sharp bone woven into or intertwined with the braids. The balls added weight to the whip, causing deep bruising and contusions as the victim was struck. The pieces of bone served to cut into the flesh. As the beating continued, the resulting cuts were so severe that the skeletal muscles, underlying veins, sinews, and bowels of victims were exposed. This beating was so severe that at times victims would not survive it in order to go on to be crucified. — *Got Questions Ministries, Got Questions? Bible Questions Answered* (Bellingham, WA: Logos Bible Software, 2002–2013).

8. **Metherell says that Jesus went into hypovolemic shock. What does that mean?**

Those who were flogged would often go into hypovolemic shock, a term that refers to low blood volume. In other words, the person would have lost so much blood he would go into shock. The results of this would be

1) The heart would race to pump blood that was not there.

2) The victim would collapse or faint due to low blood pressure.

3) The kidneys would shut down to preserve body fluids.

4) The person would experience extreme thirst as the body desired to replenish lost fluids.

There is evidence from Scripture that Jesus experienced hypovolemic shock as a result of being flogged. As Jesus carried His own cross to Golgotha (John 19:17), He collapsed, and a man named Simon was forced to either carry the cross or help Jesus carry the cross the rest of way to the hill (Matthew 27:32–33; Mark 15:21–22; Luke 23:26). This collapse indicates Jesus had low blood pressure. Another indicator that Jesus suffered from hypovolemic shock was that He declared He was thirsty as He hung on the cross (John 19:28), indicating His body's desire to replenish fluids.

Prior to death, the sustained rapid heartbeat caused by hypovolemic shock also causes fluid to gather in the sack around the heart and around the lungs. This gathering of fluid in the membrane around the heart is called pericardial effusion, and the fluid gathering around the lungs is called pleural effusion. This explains why, after Jesus died and a Roman soldier thrust a spear through Jesus' side (probably His right side, piercing both the lungs and the heart), blood and water came from His side just as John recorded in his Gospel (John 19:34). — *Got Questions Ministries, Got Questions? Bible Questions*

Answered (Bellingham, WA: Logos Bible Software, 2002–2013).

9. How does the Roman practice of crucifixion differ from modern methods of capital punishment?

"Then they crucified Him" (Matthew 27:35). Crucifixion was a form of execution that the Romans had learned from the Persians. It was also practiced in pre-Roman times in Phoenicia, Carthage, and Egypt. But it evidently originated in Persia. The Persians' believed that earth, fire, and water were sacred elements, and all customary methods of execution defiled the sacred elements. So the Persians developed a method of crucifying victims by impaling them on a pole, thus raising them high above the earth, where they were left to die. Later cultures developed different methods of crucifixion, and Rome employed several of them. By the time of Christ, crucifixion had become the favorite method of execution throughout the Roman empire, and especially in Judea, where it was regularly used to make a public example of rioters and insurrectionists. According to Josephus, after Herod the Great died, the Roman governor of Syria, Quinctilius Varus, crucified two thousand men in order to quell an uprising. Josephus also says that Titus crucified so many people when he sacked Jerusalem in A.D. 70 that there was no wood left for crosses and no place left to set them up. By the time of Christ alone, Rome had already crucified more than thirty thousand victims in and around Judea. So crosses with dead or dying men hanging on them were a common sight around Jerusalem, and a constant reminder of Roman brutality.

The exact process used in Jesus' crucifixion is a matter of some conjecture. None of the gospel accounts gives a detailed description of the method used on Him. But we can glean quite a lot of information from the incidental details that are given. From Thomas's remark to the other disciples after the crucifixion ("Unless I see in His hands the print of the nails, and put my finger into the print of the nails ... I will not believe"—John 20:25) we learn that Christ was nailed to the cross, rather than being lashed by leather thongs, as was sometimes done. From Matthew 27:37, which states that His indictment was posted "over His head," we deduce that the form of cross He was nailed to was the familiar crux imissa, where the top of the upright protruded above the patibulum, rather than the often-used St. Anthony's Cross, a T-shaped stake. — John F. MacArthur Jr., *The Murder of Jesus: A Study of How Jesus Died* (Nashville, TN: Word Publishing Group, 2000), 198–199.

10. What were the nails like?

We also can glean from secular accounts of crucifixion in Jesus' time some of the details about how crucifixion victims died. Christ would have been nailed to the cross as it lay flat on the ground. The nails used were long, tapered iron spikes, similar to modern railroad spikes, but much sharper. The nails had to be driven through the wrists (not the palms of the hands), because neither the tendons nor the bone structure in the hands could support the body's weight. Nails in the palms would simply tear the flesh between the bones. Nails through the wrists would usually shatter carpal bones and tear the carpal ligaments, but the structure of the wrist was nonetheless strong enough to support the weight of the body. As the nail went into the wrist, it would usually cause severe damage to the sensorimotor median nerve, causing intense pain in both arms. Finally, a single nail would be driven through both feet, sometimes through the Achilles' tendons. None of the nail wounds would be fatal, but they would all cause intense and increasing pain as the victim's time on the cross dragged on. — John F. MacArthur Jr., *The Murder of Jesus: A Study of How Jesus Died* (Nashville, TN: Word Publishing Group, 2000), 199.

11. What was the cross itself like?

After the victim was nailed in place, several soldiers would slowly elevate the top of the cross and carefully slide the foot into a deep posthole. The cross would drop with a jarring blow into the bottom of the hole, causing the full weight of the victim to be immediately borne by the nails in the wrists and feet. That would cause a bone-wrenching pain throughout the body, as major joints were suddenly twisted out of their natural position. That is probably what Christ referred to prophetically in Psalm 22, a psalm about the crucifixion: "I am poured out like water, and all My bones are out of joint" (v. 14). — John F. MacArthur Jr., *The Murder of Jesus: A Study of How Jesus Died* (Nashville, TN: Word Publishing Group, 2000), 199–200.

12. Why did they do crucifixion the way they did? What was the goal?

The Romans had perfected the art of crucifixion in order to maximize the pain—and they knew how to prolong the horror without permitting the victim to lapse into a state of unconsciousness that might relieve the pain. The victim of crucifixion would experience waves of nausea, fever, intense thirst, constant cramps, and incessant, throbbing pain from all parts of the body. Sleeplessness, hunger, dehydration, and worsening infection all took their toll on the victim's body and spirit as the process of crucifixion dragged on—usually for three days or so. The feeling of utter hopelessness, the public shame, and the ever-increasing trauma to the body all intensified as the hours dragged on. One author wrote,

The unnatural position made every movement painful; the lacerated veins and crushed tendons throbbed with incessant anguish; the wounds, inflamed by exposure, gradually gangrened; the arteries—especially at the head and stomach—became swollen and oppressed with surcharged blood; and while each variety of misery went on gradually increasing, there was added to them the intolerable pang of burning and raging thirst; and all these physical complications caused an internal excitement and anxiety, which made the prospect of death itself—of death, the awful unknown enemy, at whose approach man usually shudders most—bear the aspect of a delicious and exquisite release.

The emperor Tiberius is said to have preferred crucifixion as a method of punishment, precisely because it prolonged the victim's agony without granting relief by death. He believed death was an escape, so in his view execution was really no punishment, unless the victim had as much mortal agony inflicted as possible before death. — John F. MacArthur Jr., *The Murder of Jesus: A Study of How Jesus Died* (Nashville, TN: Word Publishing Group, 2000), 200–201.

13. What was that actual cause of death?

Death normally came from slow suffocation. The victim's body would hang in such a way that the diaphragm was severely constricted. In order to exhale, he would have to push up with the feet so that the diaphragm would have room to move. Ultimately fatigue, intense pain, or muscle atrophy would render the victim unable to do this, and he would finally die from the lack of oxygen. Truman Davis, a medical doctor who studied the physical effects of crucifixion, described how this would have occurred in Jesus' crucifixion:

As the arms fatigue, great waves of cramps sweep over the muscles, knotting them in deep, relentless, throbbing pain. With these cramps comes the inability to push Himself upward. Hanging by His arms, the pectoral muscles are paralyzed and the intercostal muscles are unable to act. Air can be drawn into the lungs, but cannot be exhaled. Jesus fights to raise Himself in order to get even one short breath. Finally, carbon dioxide builds up in the lungs and in the blood stream and the cramps partially subside. Spasmodically He is able to push Himself upward to exhale and bring in the life-giving oxygen... .

Hours of this limitless pain, cycles of twisting, joint-rending cramps, intermittent partial asphyxiation, searing pain as tissue is torn from His lacerated back as He moves up and down against the rough timber; then another agony begins. A deep crushing pain in the chest as the pericardium slowly fills with serum and begins to compress the heart.

It is now almost over—the loss of tissue fluid has reached a critical level—the compressed heart is struggling to pump heavy, thick, sluggish blood into the tissues—the tortured lungs are making a frantic effort to gasp in small gulps of air. The markedly dehydrated tissues send their flood of stimuli to the brain.

Once strength or feeling in the legs was gone, the victim would be unable to push up in order to breathe, and death would occur quickly. That is why the Romans sometimes practiced crucifracture—the breaking of the legs below the knees—when they wanted to hasten the process (cf. John 19:31).

Dehydration, hypovolemic shock, and congestive heart failure sometimes hastened death as well. In Jesus' case, it seems likely that acute exhaustion was probably another major contributing factor. — John F. MacArthur Jr., *The Murder of Jesus: A Study of How Jesus Died* (Nashville, TN: Word Publishing Group, 2000), 201–202.

14. John 19.33. Why didn't they break Jesus' legs?

In order to breathe while nailed to a cross, you have to visibly move your body and undergo excruciating pain. To fake death on the cross and still breathe without this being noticed would be physically impossible.

Adequate exhalation required lifting the body by pushing up on the feet and by flexing the elbows. . . . However, this would place the entire weight of the body on the tarsals and would produce searing pain. Furthermore, flexion of the elbows would cause rotation of the wrists about the iron nails and cause fiery pain along the damaged median nerves. . . . Muscle cramps and paresthesias of the outstretched and uplifted arms would add to the discomfort. As a result, each respiratory effort would become agonizing and tiring and lead eventually to asphyxia.

Thus without this physical exertion, which would be obvious to any observer, the victim would die very quickly, thus making it impossible to fake death. Soldiers would often break people's legs to speed up their death. This swoon theory has been surprisingly popular in recent years, despite its total lack of historical plausibility. — Adrian Warnock, *Raised with Christ: How the Resurrection Changes Everything* (Wheaton, IL: Crossway, 2010).

15. John 19.34. How does this detail make the swoon theory untenable?

"Clearly the weight of historical and medical evidence indicates that Jesus was dead before the wound to His side was inflicted and supports the traditional view that the spear, thrust between his right rib, probably perforated not only the right lung but also the pericardium and heart and thereby ensured His death. Accordingly, interpretations based on the assumption that Jesus did not die on the cross appear to be at odds with modern medical knowledge." Journal of the American Medical Society, March 21, 1986 — Ray Comfort, *How to Live Forever ... without Being Religious* (Orlando, FL: Bridge-Logos, 2006), 97.

16. How was Jesus' body prepared after the crucifixion? How does it make the swoon theory implausible?

In those days people would carefully prepare a body before placing it in a tomb. What they would do is put about 75 pounds of embalming ointment and spices on the body, then wrap it tight with linen cloth to form a mummy. This is all explained in John 19:39-40.

Now what I'm going to do is wrap _____ (volunteer's name) with this duct tape only on the legs. (Have volunteer sit down, and with his or her feet together, beginning at his or her ankles, wrap the duct tape around and around up to mid-calf. Make it tight, but not so tight as to cut off circulation.)

Now imagine if _____ (volunteer's name) were wrapped tight like this all the way to his or her neck. After Jesus' disciples wrapped him with the 75 pounds of ointment, it hardened like cement. So Jesus was wrapped solidly, with his legs and arms encased in the wrappings.

Now, _____ (volunteer's name), I'd like you to lie on the floor behind the chair and we are going to imagine that this is the tomb Jesus was placed in. Now this chair represents the stone door in front of Jesus' tomb. It probably weighed between one or two tons. It had to be rolled up a slotted incline by several men, and then it fell into a groove. It could be opened only from the outside. (Now ask another volunteer to come and sit on the chair that represents the stone door to the tomb.)

So there Jesus was, encased in 75 pounds of hardened spices, wrapped like a mummy, and sealed in a tomb by a stone that weighed at least one ton. Now here's what some say who think Jesus was just a normal man who never really rose from the dead. They say Jesus swooned—fainted—on the cross and just passed out. And then three days in the cold, damp tomb revived him.

Now remember, Jesus was beaten half to death and didn't have enough strength to even carry his own cross. He was nailed to the cross, and once he died, a soldier speared his side and as the Bible says, "blood and water flowed out" (John 19:34). So now the cold, damp tomb revived him, and he just wiggled his way out of his tight wrapping?

_____ (name of volunteer), why don't you try to wiggle the wrappings off your feet. You can't use your hands, because if you were in the same situation as Jesus your hands would be strapped to your side. You can't sit up either, because you would be encased in a solid mummy suit. Just try to shake your wrappings off your feet. (It will be impossible for your volunteer to do it. So continue.)

But for argument's sake, let's assume you did revive and were able to stand up in your mummy suit. (Help your volunteer to his or her feet, but keep him or her behind the chair.)

Now, _____ (volunteer's name), keep your hands to your sides and try to move this "one-ton tomb door" out of the way. (Again, your volunteer will be unable to move the chair by simply bumping it with his or her body.)

Well, it's clear here that it stretches the imagination to think that Jesus could even survive his crucifixion, let alone break out of his grave clothes and somehow move a one-ton stone door from inside the tomb. The reality is, Jesus was the Son of God who died for us and rose again from the grave because he was and is God. And his promise to give us eternal life is real! — Josh McDowell and Sean McDowell, *Resurrected—experience Freedom from the Fear of Death* (Eugene, OR: Harvest House, 2012).

17. How big was the stone that was rolled in front of Jesus grave? How much did it weigh?

Strauss raised a very important issue. Even if it was imagined that Jesus was able to survive Roman crucifixion, what could he do about the heavy stone in the entrance to the tomb? In his extremely weakened physical condition, could he move an object which even a healthy man would have a great problem with (according to tradition)? This would be even more difficult when it is remembered that the stone would have to be rolled uphill out of its gully. Additionally, the inside of the stone would provide no edge against which

Jesus might at least use his weight to push. Then, even if he could have escaped from the tomb, could he walk the distance to the disciples' hiding place after having his weight suspended on a Roman crucifixion spike just a short time previously?

Yet, Strauss' most convincing point concerned Jesus' condition upon reaching his disciples. Very few would doubt that he would be in sad physical shape, limping badly, bleeding, pale and clutching his side. He would obviously be in need of physical assistance and, at any rate, would not appear to be the resurrected and glorified Lord of Life! As Strauss pointed out, the disciples would have gone for a doctor's help rather than proclaim Jesus the risen Son of God! Strauss asserted that even if the swoon theory was conceivable, it still could not account for the disciples' belief in the risen Jesus. Since they did proclaim him to be the resurrected and glorified Lord, the swoon theory is not able to account for the facts.

Shortly after the turn of the century, Schweitzer referred to Strauss' critique as the "death-blow" to such rationalistic approaches. After Strauss' views were circulated, the liberal "lives of Jesus" usually shunned the swoon theory. By the early twentieth century, other critical scholars proclaimed this theory to be nothing more than a historical curiosity of the past. Even critics no longer considered it to be a viable hypothesis.16 — Gary R. Habermas, *The Historical Jesus: Ancient Evidence for the Life of Christ* (Joplin, MO: College Press Publishing Company, 1996), 72–73.

18. Imagine Jesus did survive the crucifixion. He is in the tomb and he wakes up. What next?

Let's just suppose for a moment that Jesus had somehow been alive in the tomb. He would have had to summon a convenient earthquake, push back the stone, fight off the soldiers who were guarding him, and then convince his disciples he was the resurrected King. His wounds and his general state of health would have made him a source of horror, not faith! Dan Story, an apologist who has written more than fifteen books, said:

There is not a shred of evidence to support this theory. Nowhere in Roman or Jewish history does anyone argue or even imply that Jesus did not die on the cross. It took eighteen centuries after Christ's death before this idea found an advocate. The fact is that the historical record refutes this theory at every turn. — Adrian Warnock, *Raised with Christ: How the Resurrection Changes Everything* (Wheaton, IL: Crossway, 2010).

19. Summary. What is the most compelling evidence against the swoon theory?

20. How can we support one another in prayer this week?

Case for Christ / Lesson #12 / Chapter 12
Was Jesus' Body Really Absent from His Tomb?
Good Questions Have Groups Talking

DIG

1. **Who read Chapter 12 this week? What got your attention?**

2. **Strobel has a great story about the first time he met William Lane Craig. Anyone remember that story?**

   I had an unusual perspective the first time I saw Bill Craig in action: I was seated behind him as he defended Christianity before a crowd of nearly eight thousand people, with countless others listening on more than one hundred radio stations across the country.

   As moderator of a debate between Craig and an atheist selected by the national spokesman for American Atheists, Inc., I marveled as Craig politely but powerfully built the case for Christianity while simultaneously dismantling the arguments for atheism. From where I was sitting, I could watch the faces of people as they discovered—many for the first time—that Christianity can stand up to rational analysis and rugged scrutiny.

   In the end it was no contest. Among those who had entered the auditorium that evening as avowed atheists, agnostics, or skeptics, an overwhelming 82 percent walked out concluding that the case for Christianity had been the most compelling. Forty-seven people entered as nonbelievers and exited as Christians—Craig's arguments for the faith were that persuasive, especially compared with the paucity of evidence for atheism. Incidentally, nobody became an atheist. — Lee Strobel, *The Case for Christ Movie Edition: Solving the Biggest Mystery of All Time* (Grand Rapids, MI: Zondervan, 2017).

3. **How important is the resurrection? Imagine we have everything else—Old Testament, Proverbs, creation story, Christmas, Paul's letters, and Revelation. But, we don't have the resurrection. How much of Christianity changes?**

The apostle Paul wrote to the Corinthians, "If Christ has not been raised, then our preaching is in vain and your faith is in vain" (1 Corinthians 15:14). The Greek word for vain refers to something that is useless or empty. Our faith means nothing if Christ is not risen from the dead.

Paul also wrote, "If Christ has not been raised, your faith is futile and you are still in your sins" (verse 17). The Greek word for futile indicates something that is without results. Our faith is meaningless if Christ is not risen.

It all boils down to this: If the resurrection of Christ did not occur, the apostles were false witnesses; our faith is vain, useless, empty, and futile; and we are all still lost in our sins. Moreover, the dead in Christ have truly perished forever, and you and I are the most pitiful people on the face of the earth—to say nothing of the fact that we have no hope beyond the grave.

The good news is that Christ is indeed risen, as we will see later in this book. For now, we simply note that Christ "presented himself alive to them after his suffering by many proofs, appearing to them during forty days and speaking about the kingdom of God"

(Acts 1:3). — Ron Rhodes, *5-Minute Apologetics for Today: 365 Quick Answers to Key Questions* (Eugene, OR: Harvest House, 2010).

4. Overview. For you, what is the most compelling evidence for the resurrection?

The evidence for the resurrection of Jesus Christ is substantial.

- The circumstances at the tomb reveal a missing body. And the Roman guards had fled their guard duty—an act punishable by the death penalty.

- Jesus appeared first to a woman, Mary Magdalene (John 20:1). In ancient Jewish culture, no one would make up a resurrection account in this way, for a woman's testimony was considered weightless.

- After the crucifixion, the disciples were full of doubt and fear. Suddenly they became willing to die for their claims. Only the resurrection explains the change.

- Only the resurrection explains the conversion of hardcore skeptics, such as the apostle Paul, James, and doubting Thomas.

- Only the resurrection explains the growth and survival of the Christian church amid Roman oppression.

- Too many appearances occurred over too many days to too many people for the resurrection to be easily dismissed (Acts 1:3).

- Jesus appeared to 500 people at one time, many of whom were still living and could have disputed Paul's resurrection claims (1 Corinthians 15:6). They did not do this, however, because the appearance of Christ was well attested.

Ron Rhodes, *5-Minute Apologetics for Today: 365 Quick Answers to Key Questions* (Eugene, OR: Harvest House, 2010).

5. 1 Corinthians 15.3 – 7. Best we can tell, when was this written?

To verify Jesus' resurrection, evidence must demonstrate that He was seen alive after His death. In Acts 1:3 Luke tells us just that—the disciples repeatedly saw Jesus over a forty-day period after His executioners pronounced Him dead and sealed His body in a tomb.

Of the twelve recorded appearances, the most stunning is Paul's claim that Jesus appeared to over five hundred eyewitnesses at one time (1 Corinthians 15:3-7). Scholars say this statement is embedded within a creed dated less than a decade after Christ's death. That early date provides great historical reliability because too little time had passed to stretch the facts. And Paul provocatively declared that most of those eye-witnesses were still alive at the time he wrote. He was apparently challenging his readers to question the witnesses to confirm his story. — Rick Cornish, *5 Minute Apologist: Maximum Truth in Minimum Time* (Colorado Springs, CO: NavPress, 2014).

6. Critics argue that the empty tomb was a legend made up by the early church. You say?

Christ's post-death appearances cannot be dismissed as nonevents. So skeptics devise other explanations to try to refute them. One option is that the witnesses lied or started a legend. But legends develop over time, and the records of Jesus' appearances occurred too soon after

the event for such legendary enhancement. Hinting that the disciples lied is extremely far-fetched because they were tortured and martyred for this belief. Someone might die for what he believes is true, but no one dies for what he knows is false. This suggestion just won't fly.
— Rick Cornish, *5 Minute Apologist: Maximum Truth in Minimum Time* (Colorado Springs, CO: NavPress, 2014).

7. Some say the early disciples hallucinated. You say?

Some propose that Jesus' followers suffered hallucinations or were highly suggestible. This view says the witnesses just saw what they wanted to believe. But ancient Jews believed the righteous dead went to heaven to await a general resurrection at the end of time. Their hallucinations would not have imagined Jesus returning to them in resurrected form because that belief was not in their theological framework. Furthermore, hallucinations are rare events that occur only to individuals, not to groups. They happen to people who expect them, but the disciples were not expecting Jesus to appear. They had lost hope and returned to their fishing business. This theory also does not explain how the disciples physically touched Jesus nor how He ate with them. And if Jesus' appearances were merely hallucinations, why didn't someone just produce the body and end the rumor?

The biblical documents claim that after His death, Jesus appeared several times to many people in different groups and situations for several weeks. Names of the witnesses and details of the encounters are listed. The accounts of physical contact with Jesus even include His crucifixion scars. The resurrection narrative is not a poorly documented fantasy, only verifiable by one or two people who could have twisted the facts. The evidence is overwhelming that Jesus was seen alive by hundreds of people after He died. His resurrection was real, it changed their lives, and it changes lives today. — Rick Cornish, *5 Minute Apologist: Maximum Truth in Minimum Time* (Colorado Springs, CO: NavPress, 2014).

8. Some say the disciples went to the wrong tomb. You say?

The wrong tomb theory states that the followers of Jesus discovered the tomb to be empty because they went to the wrong tomb. This theory has a number of problems. First, Mary Magdalene and "the other Mary" were at the tomb when Jesus was buried, so they knew which tomb to go to. Second, as if they needed a landmark, Pilate placed a number of Roman soldiers outside the tomb to prevent the body's theft. Thirdly, as mentioned above, the oldest argument against the resurrection is that the tomb was empty, which presumes the correct tomb was visited. Again we find a theory for which there is no evidence and therefore, no reason to believe. — Doug Powell, *Holman QuickSource Guide to Christian Apologetics* (Nashville, TN: Holman Reference, 2006), 280.

9. Some have said that Jesus resurrection was only of a spiritual nature, not a physical resurrection. You say?

Scripture is clear that Jesus' resurrection from the dead was physical. The resurrected Christ said to His fearful disciples, "See my hands and my feet, that it is I myself. Touch me, and see. For a spirit does not have flesh and bones as you see that I have" (Luke 24:39). Notice three things here: (1) The resurrected Christ indicates that He is not a spirit, (2) He indicates that His resurrection body is made of flesh and bones, and (3) His physical hands and feet represent physical proof of His material resurrection from the dead.

Jesus had told the Jews, "Destroy this temple, and in three days I will raise it up." The temple He was speaking about was His own body (John 2:19-21). Moreover, the resurrected Christ ate food on four different occasions to prove He had a physical body (Luke 24:30,42-43; John 21:12-13; Acts 1:4).

The resurrected Christ was touched and handled by different people (Matthew 28:9; Luke 24:39; John 20:17). Paul affirmed that the body that dies is the very same body that is raised in life (1 Corinthians 15:35-44). In the New Testament, the Greek word for body (soma), when used of a person, always means a physical body. There are no exceptions to this. So all references to Jesus' resurrection body (soma) in the New Testament must be taken to mean a resurrected physical body. — Ron Rhodes, *5-Minute Apologetics for Today: 365 Quick Answers to Key Questions* (Eugene, OR: Harvest House, 2010).

10. Matthew 27.57. Who is Joseph of Arimathea? What do we know about him?

Joseph of Arimathea was a biblical figure who played an important role in the burial of Jesus Christ. His account can be found in each of the four Gospels: Matthew 27:57–60; Mark 15:42–46; Luke 23:50–53; and John 19:38–42. He is called "Joseph of Arimathea" because "he came from the Judean town of Arimathea" (Luke 23:51) and to distinguish him from other Josephs in the Bible.

While there is not much information in the Bible about Joseph of Arimathea, there are certain things we can glean from the text. In Luke 23:50, we learn that Joseph was actually a part of the Council, or Sanhedrin—the group of Jewish religious leaders who called for Jesus' crucifixion. However, as we read on to verse 51, we see that Joseph was opposed to the Council's decision and was in fact a secret follower of Jesus (see also Mark 15:43). Joseph was a wealthy man (Matthew 27:57), although the source of his wealth is unknown. In addition, the Bible refers to Joseph as a "good and upright man" (Luke 23:50).

After Jesus' death on the cross, Joseph, at great risk to himself and his reputation, went to the Roman governor Pilate to request Jesus' body. Nicodemus, the Pharisee who had visited Jesus at night to ask questions about God's Kingdom (John 19:39; cf. John 3), accompanied Joseph. The two men were granted custody of Jesus' body, and they immediately began to prepare the body for burial. Following Jewish custom, they wrapped the body in strips of linen and mixed in myrrh and aloe. However, it was the Day of Preparation—the sixth day of the week, just before the Jewish Sabbath—and it was late in the day. So Joseph and Nicodemus hurriedly placed Jesus in Joseph's own tomb, located in a garden near the place of Jesus' crucifixion. — Got Questions Ministries, *Got Questions? Bible Questions Answered* (Bellingham, WA: Logos Bible Software, 2002–2013).

11. What prophecy did this fulfill?

Unbeknownst to Joseph and Nicodemus, their choice to put Jesus in Joseph's tomb fulfilled Isaiah's prophecy spoken hundreds of years before Jesus' death: "He was assigned a grave with the wicked, and with the rich in his death, though he had done no violence, nor was any deceit in his mouth" (Isaiah 53:9, emphasis added). This is one of the many prophecies that have confirmed Jesus' identity as the Messiah and Son of God.

The day after Jesus' burial, the chief priests and Pharisees went to Pilate to request that the stone Joseph had placed in front of the tomb be sealed, and a guard

posted, for three days. They cited Jesus' assertion that
He would rise after three days and claimed the disciples
might attempt to steal the body in order to fabricate
a resurrection (Matthew 27:63–64). Their precautions
were for naught, as Jesus rose from the dead on the
third day, just as He had predicted (Matthew 28). — Got
Questions Ministries, *Got Questions? Bible Questions
Answered* (Bellingham, WA: Logos Bible Software, 2002–
2013).

12. What did the tomb of Jesus look like?

Concerning that which covered the opening of Jesus'
tomb, A. B. Bruce says: "The Jews called the stone golel"
(Bruce, EGNT, 334).

H. W. Holloman, citing G. M. Mackie, says: "The opening
to the central chamber was guarded by a large and
heavy disc of rock which could roll along a groove slightly
depressed at the centre, in front of the tomb entrance"
(Holloman, EPR, 38).

T. J. Thorburn mentions that this stone was used "as a
protection against both men and beasts." He further
observes: "This stone is often mentioned by the
Talmudists. According to Maimonides, a structure ex
lingo, alia Materia was also used." Of the enormous
size of such a stone Dr. Thorburn comments: "It usually
required several men to remove it." Since the one rolled
to the entrance of Jesus' tomb was intended to prevent
an expected theft, it was probably even larger than
what would normally have been used (Thorburn, RNMC,
97–98)!

Indeed, concerning the tremendous weight of the
rock, Thorburn remarks: "A gloss in Cod. Bez. [a phrase
written in parenthesis, within the text of Mark 16:4 as
found in a fourth-century manuscript (Codex Bezae in

the Cambridge Library)] adds, 'And when he was laid there, he [Joseph] put against the tomb a stone which twenty men could not roll away.' " The significance of Dr. Thorburn's observation is realized when one considers the rules for transcribing manuscripts. It was the custom that if a copier was emphasizing his own interpretation, he would write his thought in the margin and not include it within the text. One might conclude, therefore, that the insert in the text was copied from a text even closer to the time of Christ, perhaps a first century manuscript. The phrase, then, could have been recorded by an eyewitness who was impressed with the enormity of the stone that was rolled against Jesus' sepulchre. Gilbert West of Oxford also brings out the importance of this portion of the Bezae Codex on pages 37 and 38 of his work Observations on the History and Evidences of the Resurrection of Jesus Christ (Thorburn, RNMC, 1–2). — Josh McDowell, *Evidence for Christianity* (Nashville, TN: Thomas Nelson Publishers, 2006), 283–284.

13. What did the stone look like? How big was it? How heavy was it?

This tomb was probably a man-made cave cut out of one of the many limestone hills in the area around Jerusalem. It was large enough to walk into (John 20:6). Matthew records that this was Joseph's own previously unused tomb (Matthew 27:60). Joseph and Nicodemus wrapped Jesus' body, placed it in the tomb, and rolled a heavy stone across the entrance. The religious leaders also watched where Jesus was buried. They stationed guards by the tomb and sealed the stone to make sure that no one would steal Jesus' body and claim he had risen from the dead (Matthew 27:62–66). All of these actions give us verification that Jesus truly had died. — Bruce B. Barton, *Mark, Life Application Bible*

Commentary (Wheaton, IL: Tyndale House Publishers, 1994), 473–474.

14. What do we know about the guards that protected Jesus' tomb?

Understanding who these guards were, as previously discussed makes the narrative of Matthew 28 very impressive. The sight that coincided with Jesus' resurrection was frightening enough to cause rugged soldiers to "become like dead men" (Matt. 28:4).

Thomas Thorburn tells us that the guard that had kept the watch was in dire straits. After the stone had been rolled away and the seal broken, they were as good as court-martialed. Thorburn writes: "The soldiers cannot have alleged they were asleep, for they well knew that the penalty of sleeping upon a watch was death—always rigorously enforced" (Thorburn, RNMC, 179–82).

Thorburn continues: "Here the soldiers would have practically no other alternative than to trust to the good offices of the priests. The body (we will suppose) was gone, and their negligence in any case would (under ordinary circumstances) be punishable by death (cp. Acts xii. 19)" (Thorburn, RNMC, 179–82). — Josh McDowell, *Evidence for Christianity* (Nashville, TN: Thomas Nelson Publishers, 2006), 304.

15. What about the seal? What do we know about that?

A. T. Robertson comments: "The sealing was done in the presence of the Roman guard who were left in charge to protect this stamp of Roman authority and power" (Robertson, WPNT, 239).

D. D. Whedon says: "The door could not be opened, therefore, without breaking the seal; which was a crime against the authority of the proprietor of the seal" (Whedon, CGM, 343).

The seal was broken when the stone was rolled away. The person or persons who were responsible for breaking the seal would have the provincial governor and his agencies to answer to. Indeed, at the time of Christ's resurrection, everyone feared the breaking of the Roman seal. — Josh McDowell, (Nashville, TN: Thomas Nelson Publishers, 2006), 303.

16. Some have argued that the resurrection accounts have so many contradictions that they are impossible to harmonize. You say?

The four Gospels have unique perspectives but not actual contradictions.

If all four Gospels were virtually the same, critics would say the writers colluded. The differences in the Gospels show that the writers did not collude but rather represented four different but equally inspired accounts of the same events.

A partial account in a Gospel is not a faulty account. In Matthew 27:5, for example, we learn that Judas died by hanging himself. In Acts 1:18, we find that Judas burst open in the middle, and all his entrails gushed out. These are both partial accounts. Neither account gives us the full picture. But taken together we can easily reconstruct how Judas died. He hanged himself, and sometime later, the rope loosened, and Judas fell to the rocks below, thereby causing his intestines to gush out.

Many alleged contradictions are solved by following proper hermeneutics, like these:

- Remember that the Bible typically uses nontechnical, everyday language.

- Interpret the Old Testament in light of the New Testament.

- Interpret the difficult verses in light of the clear verses.

- Remember that the Bible does not approve of everything it records (such as the words of Satan).

Ron Rhodes, *5-Minute Apologetics for Today: 365 Quick Answers to Key Questions* (Eugene, OR: Harvest House, 2010).

17. Does the women's relationship with Jesus call the reliability of their testimony into question?

Unwittingly, I had played right into Craig's hand. "Actually, this argument backfires on people who use it," Craig said in response. "Certainly these women were friends of Jesus. But when you understand the role of women in first-century Jewish society, what's really extraordinary is that this empty tomb story should feature women as the discoverers of the empty tomb in the first place.

"Women were on a very low rung of the social ladder in first-century Palestine. There are old rabbinical sayings that said, 'Let the words of the Law be burned rather than delivered to women' and 'Blessed is he whose children are male, but woe to him whose children are female.' Women's testimony was regarded as so worthless that they weren't generally allowed to serve as legal witnesses in a Jewish court of law.

"In light of this, it's absolutely remarkable that the chief witnesses to the empty tomb are these women who were friends of Jesus. Any later legendary account would have certainly portrayed male disciples as discovering the tomb—Peter or John, for example. The fact that women are the first witnesses to the empty tomb is most plausibly explained by the reality that—like it or not—they were the discoverers of the empty tomb! This shows that the gospel writers faithfully recorded what happened, even if it was embarrassing. This bespeaks the historicity of this tradition rather than its legendary status." — Lee Strobel, *The Case for Christ Movie Edition: Solving the Biggest Mystery of All Time* (Grand Rapids, MI: Zondervan, 2017).

18. How was life for women different in the first century as compare with today?

All four Gospels say women were the first witnesses of the empty tomb and the first to learn of the Resurrection. One of those women was Mary Magdalene, who Luke admits had been demon-possessed (Luke 8:2). This would never be inserted in a made-up story. Not only would a once-demon-possessed person make a questionable witness, but women in general were not considered reliable witnesses in that first-century culture. In fact, a woman's testimony carried no weight in a court of law. So if you were making up a resurrection story in the first century, you would avoid women witnesses and make yourselves—the brave men—the first ones to discover the empty tomb and the risen Jesus. Citing the testimony of women—especially demon-possessed women—would only hurt your attempt to pass off a lie as the truth. — Norman L. Geisler and Frank Turek, *I Don't Have Enough Faith to Be an Atheist* (Wheaton, IL: Crossway Books, 2004), 282.

19. Summary. What do we know for sure about the resurrection?

Gary Habermas has completed the most comprehensive investigation to date on what scholars believe about the Resurrection. Habermas collected more than 1,400 of the most critical scholarly works on the Resurrection written from 1975 to 2003. In The Risen Jesus and Future Hope, Habermas reports that virtually all scholars from across the ideological spectrum—from ultra-liberals to Bible-thumping conservatives—agree that the following points concerning Jesus and Christianity are actual historical facts:

1. Jesus died by Roman crucifixion.

2. He was buried, most likely in a private tomb.

3. Soon afterwards the disciples were discouraged, bereaved, and despondent, having lost hope.

4. Jesus' tomb was found empty very soon after his interment.

5. The disciples had experiences that they believed were actual appearances of the risen Jesus.

6. Due to these experiences, the disciples' lives were thoroughly transformed. They were even willing to die for their belief.

7. The proclamation of the Resurrection took place very early, from the beginning of church history.

8. The disciples' public testimony and preaching of the Resurrection took place in the city of Jerusalem, where Jesus had been crucified and buried shortly before.

9. The gospel message centered on the preaching of the death and resurrection of Jesus.

10. Sunday was the primary day for gathering and worshiping.

11. James, the brother of Jesus and a skeptic before this time, was converted when he believed he also saw the risen Jesus.

12. Just a few years later, Saul of Tarsus (Paul) became a Christian believer, due to an experience that he also believed was an appearance of the risen Jesus.

Norman L. Geisler and Frank Turek, *I Don't Have Enough Faith to Be an Atheist* (Wheaton, IL: Crossway Books, 2004), 298–300.

20. How can we pray for each other this week?

Case for Christ / Lesson #13
Chapters 13 & 14
Was Jesus Seen Alive after His Death on the Cross?
Are There Any Supporting Facts That Point to the Resurrection?
Good Questions Have Groups Talking
www.joshhunt.com

DIG

1. Who read Chapters 13 & 14 this week? What got your attention?

2. Critics point out that no one witnessed the resurrection. You say?

"That's exactly right—there's no descriptive account of the resurrection," Habermas replied in an admission that might surprise people who only have a casual knowledge of the subject.

"When I was young, I was reading a book by C. S. Lewis, who wrote that the New Testament says nothing about the resurrection. I wrote a real big 'No!' in the margin. Then I realized what he was saying: Nobody was sitting inside the tomb and saw the body start to vibrate, stand up, take the linen wrappings off, fold them, roll back the stone, wow the guards, and leave."

That, it seemed to me, might pose some problems. "Doesn't this hurt your efforts to establish that the resurrection is a historical event?" I asked.

Habermas pushed back his chair to get more comfortable. "No, this doesn't hurt our case one iota, because science is all about causes and effects. We don't see dinosaurs; we study the fossils. We may not know how a disease originates, but we study its symptoms. Maybe nobody witnesses a crime, but police piece together the evidence after the fact.

"So," he continued, "here's how I look at the evidence for the resurrection: First, did Jesus die on the cross? And second, did he appear later to people? If you can establish those two things, you've made your case, because dead people don't normally do that."

Historians agree there's plenty of evidence that Jesus was crucified, and Dr. Alexander Metherell demonstrated in an earlier chapter that Jesus could not have survived the rigors of that execution. That leaves the second part of the issue: Did Jesus really appear later? — Lee Strobel, *The Case for Christ Movie Edition: Solving the Biggest Mystery of All Time* (Grand Rapids, MI: Zondervan, 2017).

3. **1 Corinthians 15.3 – 8. Best we can tell, about when was this written?**

Note the fascinating timeline: Paul, who had visited Corinth in AD 51 (cf. Acts 18), wrote around AD 55 that he had "delivered" to the Corinthians the tradition he himself had "received" from the first witnesses of Jesus' life, death, and resurrection (see 1 Corinthians 15:3–8). Now, the majority of scholars—liberal or conservative—hold that Paul "received" this tradition from James, "the Lord's brother," three years after Paul's conversion

(Galatians 1:18), discussing for fifteen days Christianity's foundational historical events; Paul's conversion was two to three years after Jesus' death. Paul immediately assures us the facts are utterly true (1:20).

In sum, we have a very early Jerusalem tradition about Jesus' life, death, and resurrection that goes back to the earliest Christian preaching shortly after the first Easter. James Dunn estimates the formalized tradition dates to within two years of Jesus' death, and even the liberal German critic Gerd Lüdemann affirms that "the elements in the tradition are to be dated to the first two years after the crucifixion ... not later than three years after the death of Jesus." Contrary to John Hick, the gospel message didn't take a long time to "evolve"19 but was implicit from the outset, contained in the earliest Christian proclamations, such as "Jesus is Lord." — Paul Copan, *"True for You but Not for Me"* (Minneapolis, MN: Bethany House, 2009), 157–158.

4. How many witnesses to the risen Christ are listed in this passage?

To verify Jesus' resurrection, evidence must demonstrate that He was seen alive after His death. In Acts 1:3 Luke tells us just that—the disciples repeatedly saw Jesus over a forty-day period after His executioners pronounced Him dead and sealed His body in a tomb.

Of the twelve recorded appearances, the most stunning is Paul's claim that Jesus appeared to over five hundred eyewitnesses at one time (1 Corinthians 15:3-7). Scholars say this statement is embedded within a creed dated less than a decade after Christ's death. That early date provides great historical reliability because too little time had passed to stretch the facts. And Paul provocatively declared that most of those eye-witnesses were still alive at the time he wrote. He was apparently challenging his readers to question the witnesses to confirm his story. — Rick Cornish, *5 Minute Apologist: Maximum Truth in Minimum Time* (Colorado Springs, CO: NavPress, 2014).

5. What does Paul mean that he is abnormally born?

Paul's inclusion of himself does not suggest that he needed to defend his apostleship to the Corinthians, but it affords him an opportunity to stress the gracious character of God's call and its effect on his own life (15:10). Paul calls himself a "miscarried child" (ektrōma; NIV: "abnormally born"), a term that refers to a premature birth or miscarriage, where the child, if surviving, could be severely handicapped.5 God's grace alone has made Paul worth more than a dead corpse (cf. Num. 12:12; Job 3:16; Eccles. 6:3). Paul's unworthiness as an apostle is displayed by his life before his encounter with the resurrected Christ: he "persecuted the church of God." — Preben Vang, *1 Corinthians*, ed. Mark L. Strauss, *Teach the Text Commentary Series* (Grand Rapids, MI: Baker Books, 2014), 202.

6. Habermas lists several post-resurrection appearances of Christ. Let's see how many we can recall.

I started this line of inquiry by asking Habermas to describe the post-resurrection appearances in Matthew, Mark, Luke, and John.

"There are several different appearances to a lot of different people in the gospels and Acts—some individually, some in groups, sometimes indoors, sometimes outdoors, to softhearted people like John and skeptical people like Thomas," he began.

"At times they touched Jesus or ate with him, with the texts teaching that he was physically present. The appearances occurred over several weeks. And there are good reasons to trust these accounts—for example, they're lacking in many typical mythical tendencies."

"Can you enumerate these appearances for me?"

From memory, Habermas described them one at a time. Jesus appeared

- to Mary Magdalene, in John 20:10–18;

- to the other women, in Matthew 28:8–10;

- to Cleopas and another disciple on the road to Emmaus, in Luke 24:13–32;

- to eleven disciples and others, in Luke 24:33–49;

- to ten apostles and others, with Thomas absent, in John 20:19–23;

- to Thomas and the other apostles, in John 20:26–30;

- to seven apostles, in John 21:1–14;

- to the disciples, in Matthew 28:16–20.

- And he was with the apostles at the Mount of Olives before his ascension, in Luke 24:50–52 and Acts 1:4–9.

"It's particularly interesting," Habermas added, "that C. H. Dodd, the Cambridge University scholar, has carefully analyzed these appearances and concluded that several of them are based on especially early material, including Jesus' encounter with the women, in Matthew 28:8–10; his meeting with the eleven apostles, in which he gave them the Great Commission, in Matthew 28:16–20;

and his meeting with the disciples, in John 20:19–23, in which he showed them his hands and side." — Lee Strobel, *The Case for Christ Movie Edition: Solving the Biggest Mystery of All Time* (Grand Rapids, MI: Zondervan, 2017).

7. **Let's skip to the next chapter—what Strobel calls Exhibit #1 The Disciples Died for their Beliefs. How does this help to prove the resurrection?**

Dr. Peterson took a sip of his lemonade and continued, "Brett, I have looked into every possibility, and the resurrection is the best explanation in light of the abundance of evidence. After the resurrection, eleven of the twelve apostles were martyred—not just because of something they believed in, but for something they knew to be true. People may die for a lie they think is true, but they won't die for a lie they know to be false. Last year, when I was still skeptical and reading from the leading scholars on this subject, I remember reading from Dr. Peter Kreeft, a professor of philosophy at Boston College. He asked, 'Why would the apostles lie? ... If they lied, what was their motive, what did they get out of this? What they got out of it was misunderstanding, rejection, persecution, torture, and martyrdom. Hardly a list of perks.'" — Josh McDowell and Dave Sterrett, *Coffee House Chronicles Set* (Chicago, IL: Moody Publishers, 2011).

8. **Imagine the disciples stole the body and made up the story of the resurrection. Soon, heavy persecution comes. What do you imagine would happen to these disciples when the heat was turned up?**

Finally, in addition to abandoning long-held sacred institutions and adopting new ones, the New Testament writers suffered persecution and death when they could have saved themselves by recanting. If they had made up the Resurrection story, they certainly would have said so when they were about to be crucified (Peter), stoned (James), or beheaded (Paul). But no one recanted— eleven out of the twelve were martyred for their faith (the only survivor was John, who was exiled to the Greek island of Patmos). Why would they die for a known lie?

Chuck Colson, former aide to President Nixon and founder of Prison Fellowship, went to prison over the Watergate scandal. Comparing his experience to that of the apostles, he writes,

> Watergate involved a conspiracy to cover up, perpetuated by the closest aides to the President of the United States—the most powerful men in America, who were intensely loyal to their president. But one of them, John Dean, turned state's evidence, that is, testified against Nixon, as he put it, "to save his own skin"—and he did so only two weeks after informing the president about what was really going on—two weeks! The real cover-up, the lie, could only be held together for two weeks, and then everybody else jumped ship in order to save themselves. Now, the fact is that all that those around the president were facing was embarrassment, maybe prison. Nobody's life was at stake. But what about the disciples? Twelve powerless men, peasants really, were facing not just embarrassment or political disgrace, but beatings, stonings, execution. Every single one of the disciples insisted, to their dying breaths, that they had physically seen Jesus bodily raised from the dead. Don't you think that one of those apostles would have cracked before being beheaded or stoned? That one of them would have made a deal with the authorities? None did.

Colson is right. The apostles surely would have cracked to save themselves. Peter had already denied Jesus three times before the Resurrection in order to "save his skin"! He surely would have denied him after the Resurrection if the story had turned out to be a hoax. — Norman L. Geisler and Frank Turek, *I Don't Have Enough Faith to Be an Atheist* (Wheaton, IL: Crossway Books, 2004), 292–293.

9. But, don't Muslims martyr themselves all the time? What does it prove the early disciples were martyred?

When people discuss the beliefs of Jesus' disciples and their willingness to suffer martyrdom for their convictions, they often make comparisons to other religious persons whose lives were also changed due to their own religious beliefs. Like Jesus' disciples, many have willingly given their lives for their beliefs. Examples include modern Muslims, the followers of various religious teachers, and certain UFO groups. Even political ideas, such as communism, have inspired life changes and martyrdoms.

Under these circumstances, can Christians continue to make evidential use of the disciples' transformations?

Initially, we need to make a crucial distinction. Transformed lives, whether the disciples' or others', do not prove that someone's teachings are true. However, they do constitute evidence that those who are willing to suffer and die for their religious commitments truly believe them to be true.

So, can we distinguish between the disciples' transformations and the experiences of others? In general, people committed to a religious or political message really believe it to be true. Of course, beliefs can be false. But in the case of Jesus' disciples, one grand distinction makes all the difference in the world.

Like other examples of religious or political faith, the disciples believed and followed their leader's teachings. But unlike all others, the disciples had more than just their beliefs—they had seen the resurrected Jesus. This is a crucial distinction; their faith was true precisely because of the resurrection. — Gary R. Habermas, "How Is the Transformation of Jesus' Disciples Different from Other Religious Transformations?," in *The Apologetics Study Bible: Real Questions, Straight Answers, Stronger Faith*, ed. Ted Cabal et al. (Nashville, TN: Holman Bible Publishers, 2007), 1565.

10. Exhibit #2 is the conversion of skeptics. What are some examples of skeptics who came to believe?

The next fourteen centuries contain numerous additional testimonies of converted skeptics.

In the mid-eighteenth century **Lord George Lyttleton** (a member of Parliament and Commissioner of the Treasury) and Gilbert West, Esq., went to Oxford. There, they were determined to attack the very basis of Christianity. Lyttleton set out to prove that Saul of Tarsus was never really converted to Christianity, and West intended to demonstrate that Jesus never really rose from the dead.

Each had planned to do a painstaking job, taking a year to establish their case. But as they proceeded, they eventually concluded that Christianity was true. Both became Christians.

West eventually wrote Observations on the History and Evidences of the Resurrection of Jesus Christ (1747). George Lyttleton wrote a lengthy text titled The

Conversion of St. Paul (rpt. 1929).Their correspondence back and forth, showing their surprise at the quality of the evidence, can be found in any university library (Early American Imprints #8909 (1639-1800) of the American Antiquarian Society). West became totally convinced of the truth of the Resurrection, and Lyttleton of the genuine conversion of Saint Paul on the basis of it.

For example, Lyttleton wrote to West in 1761, [page 3 of #8909 above]:

> Sir, in a late conversation we had together upon the subject of the Christian religion, I told you that besides all the proofs of it which may be drawn from the prophecies of the Old Testament, from the necessary connection it has with the whole system of the Jewish religion, from the miracles of Christ, and from the evidence given of his reflection by all the other apostles, I thought the conversion and apostleship of Saint Paul alone, duly considered, was of itself a demonstration sufficient to prove Christianity a divine revelation.

Lyttleton, the skeptic, wrote over seventy pages of data confirming the conversion of Saul and the reliability of his New Testament writings.

In our own century, the conversion of skeptics and doubters has continued. In the 1930's a rationalistic English journalist named **Frank Morison** attempted to discover the "real" Jesus Christ. He was convinced that Christ's "history rested upon very insecure foundations"—largely because of the influence of the rationalistic higher criticism so prevalent in his day (99:9-10). Further, he was dogmatically opposed to the miraculous elements in the Gospels. But he was nevertheless fascinated by the person of Jesus, who was to him "an almost legendary figure of purity and noble manhood" (99:10).

Morison decided to take the crucial "last phase" in the life of Christ and "to strip it of its overgrowth of primitive beliefs and dogmatic suppositions, and to see this supremely great Person as he really was" (99:11). "It seemed to me that if I could come at the truth why this man died a cruel death at the hands of the Roman Power, how he himself regarded the matter, and especially how he behaved under the test, I should be very near to the true solution of the problem" (99:11).

But the book that Morison ended up writing was not the one he intended to. He came to believe that the "miraculous elements" in the Gospels were sober history. He proceeded to write one of the most able defenses of the Resurrection of Christ in our time titled Who Moved the Stone? (99). The evidence he encountered for the Resurrection of Christ had changed his initial skepticism and proceeded to change his entire life.

Dr. Cyril E. M. Joad, head of the Philosophy Department at the University of London, once believed that Jesus was only a man. For many years, he was an antagonist toward Christianity. But near the end of his life he came to believe that the only solution for mankind was "found in the cross of Jesus Christ." He became a zealous follower of Christ (52:342).

Giovanni Papine was one of the foremost Italian intellects of his period, an atheist and vocal enemy of the church and self-appointed debunker of religion. But he became converted to faith in Christ and in 1921 penned his Life of Christ, stunning most of his friends and admirers (52:357).

The Cambridge scholar **C. S. Lewis**, a former atheist, was converted to Christianity on the basis of the evidence according to his text Surprised by Joy. He recalls, "I thought I had the Christians 'placed' and disposed of forever" (259:175). But, "A young man who wishes to remain a sound atheist cannot be too careful of his reading. There are traps everywhere—`Bibles laid open, millions of surprises,' as Herbert says, 'Fine nets and stratagems.' God is, if I may say it, very unscrupulous" (259:191).

But **C. S. Lewis** became a Christian because the evidence was compelling and he could not escape it. Even against his will he was "brought in kicking, struggling, resentful, and darting [my] eyes in every direction for a chance of escape" (259:229). The God "whom I so earnestly desired not to meet" became His Lord and Savior (259:228). His book on Christian evidences, Mere Christianity, is considered a classic and has been responsible for converting thousands to the faith, among them former skeptic and Watergate figure Charles Colson, author of Born Again.

As a pre-law student, **Josh McDowell** was also skeptical of Christianity and believed that every Christian had two minds: one was lost, the other was out looking for it. Eventually challenged to intellectually investigate the Christian truth claims and thinking this a farce, he accepted the challenge and "as a result, I found historical facts and evidence about Jesus Christ that I never knew existed" (52:373). He eventually wrote a number of important texts in defense of Christianity, among them Evidence That Demands a Verdict, More Evidence That Demands a Verdict, More Than a Carpenter and Daniel in the Lion's Den.

Dr. Gary Habermas was raised a Christian. But he soon questioned his faith. He concluded that while the Resurrection could be believed, he personally doubted it and was skeptical that any evidence for it was convincing. But eventually it was the evidence that brought him around and he concluded the Resurrection was an established historic fact (254). He proceeded to write four books in defense of the Resurrection: Ancient Evidence For the Life of Jesus; The Resurrection of Jesus: A Rational Inquiry; The Resurrection of Jesus: An Apologetic; and Did Jesus Rise From the Dead: The Resurrection Debate (11; 203-5). — John Ankerberg and John Weldon, *Do the Resurrection Accounts Conflict and What Proof Is There That Jesus Rose from the Dead?* (Chattanooga, TN: ATRI Publishing, 2011).

11. Exhibit #3. How is our world different—and better—because of the Christian faith?

Even knowledgeable believers will be amazed at how many of our present institutions and values reflect a Christian origin. Not only countless individual lives but civilization itself was transformed by Jesus Christ. In the ancient world, His teachings elevated brutish standards of morality, halted infanticide, enhanced human life, emancipated women, abolished slavery, inspired charities and relief organizations, created hospitals, established orphanages, and founded schools.

In medieval times, Christianity almost single-handedly kept classical culture alive through recopying manuscripts, building libraries, moderating warfare through truce days, and providing dispute arbitration. It was Christians who invented colleges and universities, dignified labor as a divine vocation, and extended the light of civilization to barbarians on the frontiers.

In the modern era, Christian teaching, properly expressed, advanced science, instilled concepts of political and social and economic freedom, fostered justice, and provided the greatest single source of inspiration for the magnificent achievements in art, architecture, music, and literature that we treasure to this present day. . . . No other religion, philosophy, teaching, nation, movement—whatever—has so changed the world for the better as Christianity has done.113—Paul Maier in How Christianity Changed the World by Alvin J. Schmidt. — Robert J. Morgan, *100 Bible Verses Everyone Should Know by Heart* (Nashville: B&H, 2010).

12. How does Moreland think that communion can be used as circumstantial evidence to the resurrection?

"Isn't it only natural that religions would create their own rituals and practices?" I asked. "All religions have them. So how does that prove anything about the resurrection?"

"Ah, but let's consider Communion for a moment," he replied. "What's odd is that these early followers of Jesus didn't get together to celebrate his teachings or how wonderful he was. They came together regularly to have a celebration meal for one reason: to remember that Jesus had been publicly slaughtered in a grotesque and humiliating way.

"Think about this in modern terms. If a group of people loved John F. Kennedy, they might meet regularly to remember his confrontation with Russia, his promotion of civil rights, and his charismatic personality. But they're not going to celebrate the fact that Lee Harvey Oswald murdered him!

"However, that's analogous to what these early Christians did. How do you explain that? I explain it this way: They realized that Jesus' slaying was a necessary step to a much greater victory. His murder wasn't the last word—the last word was that he had conquered death for all of us by rising from the dead. They celebrated his execution because they were convinced that they had seen him alive from the tomb." — Lee Strobel, *The Case for Christ Movie Edition: Solving the Biggest Mystery of All Time* (Grand Rapids, MI: Zondervan, 2017).

13. What about Baptism?

"The early church adopted a form of baptism from their Jewish upbringing, called proselyte baptism. When Gentiles wanted to take upon themselves the laws of Moses, the Jews would baptize those Gentiles in the authority of the God of Israel. But in the New Testament, people were baptized in the name of God the Father, God the Son, and God the Holy Spirit—which meant they had elevated Jesus to the full status of God.

"Not only that, but baptism was a celebration of the death of Jesus, just as Communion was. By going under the water, you're celebrating his death, and by being brought out of the water, you're celebrating the fact that Jesus was raised to newness of life."

I interrupted by saying, "You're assuming that these sacraments weren't merely adapted from the so-called mystery religions."

"And for good reasons," Moreland replied. "First, there's no hard evidence that any mystery religion believed in gods dying and rising, until after the New Testament period. So if there was any borrowing, they borrowed from Christianity.

"Second, the practice of baptism came from Jewish customs, and the Jews were very much against allowing Gentile or Greek ideas to affect their worship. And third, these two sacraments can be dated back to the very earliest Christian community—too early for the influence of any other religions to creep into their understanding of what Jesus' death meant." — Lee Strobel, *The Case for Christ Movie Edition: Solving the Biggest Mystery of All Time* (Grand Rapids, MI: Zondervan, 2017).

14. How is the emergence of the church circumstantial evidence to the resurrection?

Apart from the resurrection, it's hard to explain the beginnings of the church, which emerged in the very city where Jesus had been crucified a few weeks earlier. The church grew out of the claim that he had come back to life. If false, it could have been easily disproven. — Lee Strobel and Mark Mittelberg, *Moments of Truth* (Grand Rapids, MI: Zondervan, 2016).

15. Let's summarize. Why do you believe in God, in Jesus, in the resurrection?

The majority of human beings who have ever lived would say that atheists Bertrand Russell, Christopher Hitchens, Richard Dawkins, Sam Harris, and Daniel Dennett are wrong. The best minds in the history of the human race — Plato, Augustine, Aquinas, Newton, Descartes, Leibniz, Pascal, Kierkegaard — thought that there were good reasons to believe there is a God. Since none of them are around to write out an explanation of why they believe, I will have to suffice.

And here is how I would like to lay it out. We will sift through a number of reasons to believe in God, looking for the one best reason.

G. K. Chesterton wrote:

> If I am asked why I believe in Christianity, I can only answer, "for the same reason that an intelligent agnostic disbelieves in Christianity." I believe in it quite rationally upon the evidence. But that evidence . . . is not really in this or that alleged demonstration, it is in an enormous accumulation of small but unanimous facts. In fact, the secularist is not to be blamed because his objections to Christianity are miscellaneous and even scrappy; it is precisely such scrappy evidence that does convince the mind.

— John Ortberg, *Know Doubt: Embracing Uncertainty in Your Faith* (Grand Rapids, MI: Zondervan, 2014).

16. C.S. Lewis taught that in every argument—about anything—is a hidden proof for the existence of God. What did he mean by that?

I believe we have a moral code in our hearts and that Somebody put it there. This idea comes by way of C. S. Lewis.

Pay attention the next time you hear an argument. Maybe you can go start one just to check this out. Nancy and I had a good argument recently about which one of us was supposed to buy a clock radio for me. Surprisingly, I lost.

When people argue, here are the kinds of things they say:

"I do way more than my fair share of work around this house, and you do way too little!" We call those people husbands and wives.

"He got a bigger piece of dessert. He got a bigger allowance! He did fewer chores. He got a later curfew time than I did, and it's not fair!" We call those people brothers and sisters.

"You're a miserable boss, and this is a dysfunctional sweat shop, and I am grossly overworked and criminally underpaid." We call those people unemployed.

When we argue, we don't just say, "Do what I want because I'm stronger and I can make you do it." We say things like, "That's not right! That's not good! You're not being fair!" In other words, we appeal to a standard that is independent and objective and higher than you and I. We appeal to the idea that there is such a thing as right and wrong.

In theory, many people in our day hold the belief that right and wrong are subjective — just preference, just vanilla and chocolate. You have yours, and I have mine. Everybody is different. Author Dinesh D'Souza points out that in our society we will often hear someone say, "Don't impose your beliefs on me."

D'Souza says he finds it interesting that we don't say, "Don't impose your geometry on me. Don't impose your chemistry on me." Why don't we hear such things? Because we assume that science and mathematics are about objective reality. We don't think they can be "imposed" on us. But we often believe that morals and values are simply subjective preferences. You have yours. I have mine. Everything is arbitrary. Whenever you hear two people argue about whether something is right or wrong, it shows we know that right or wrong isn't subjective. Deep down we all live on the assumption that moral reality is built into the way life is.

This is exactly what Paul was writing about when he said that "the requirements of the law [what's right and what's wrong] are written on [people's] hearts." We can't get away from this. When we argue, we show that we know this. Paul continues, "their consciences also bearing witness, and their thoughts now accusing, now even defending them" (Romans 2:15).

Every human being knows two things: There is a way we ought to behave. We do not invent this code; we only discover it. We might be fuzzy on the details of it sometimes, but we have a general idea of what it is. We also know that we don't live up to this standard. We all fall short. We need forgiveness. We need grace. We need to get fixed.

Every time people argue, they are implying that the universe is not an accident, that there is a moral order built into the way things are, because it was put there by Somebody, and that Somebody is God. The good news is that he is a gracious God. That's part of why I believe in God. But it's not the main reason. — John Ortberg, *Know Doubt: Embracing Uncertainty in Your Faith* (Grand Rapids, MI: Zondervan, 2014).

17. John Ortberg says that banana cream pie proves the existence of God. Anyone want to make a guess as to what that is about?

I had a philosophy professor in college named Steve Evans, and although I often couldn't keep up with him, he made one statement I have never forgotten: one of the greatest proofs of the existence of God is banana cream pie. It's kind of a shorthand version of the claim that we can reason from the existence of creation to the existence of a Creator.

What is convincing to me about that is not simply the complexity of creation. I know some people argue that the complexity of, for example, the human eye can only be explained by a creator. For me, complexity does not get to the root of the matter. And I get a little concerned about a "God of the gaps" approach that requires science or natural selection to be unable to account for something in order to prove God. What if down the road science figures it out?

No, what is convincing to me is not so much the complexity of creation as the goodness of creation. If there is no God, then it really doesn't matter if anything exists or not. But there is another way of viewing things: "God spoke, and it was so, and God saw that it was good." Even the ugliness we see — cancer and pollution and slums — are painful precisely because creation is so good when it is right. The goodness of creation is a reason to believe. But it is not the greatest reason. — John Ortberg, *Know Doubt: Embracing Uncertainty in Your Faith* (Grand Rapids, MI: Zondervan, 2014).

18. Pascal offered a reason to believe in God. It has come to be known as Pascal's wager. Anyone know what that is about?

Pascal's Wager is named after 17th-century French philosopher and mathematician Blaise Pascal. One of Pascal's most famous works was the Pensées ("Thoughts"), which was published posthumously in 1670. It is in this work that we find what is known as Pascal's Wager.

The gist of the Wager is that, according to Pascal, one cannot come to the knowledge of God's existence through reason alone, so the wise thing to do is to live your life as if God does exist because such a life has everything to gain and nothing to lose. If we live as though God exists, and He does indeed exist, we have gained heaven. If He doesn't exist, we have lost nothing. If, on the other hand, we live as though God does not exist and He really does exist, we have gained hell and punishment and have lost heaven and bliss. If one weighs the options, clearly the rational choice to live as if God exists is the better of the possible choices. Pascal even suggested that some may not, at the time, have the ability to believe in God. In such a case, one should live as if he had faith anyway. Perhaps living as if one had faith may lead one to actually come to faith. — Got Questions Ministries, Got Questions? *Bible Questions Answered* (Bellingham, WA: Logos Bible Software, 2002–2013).

19. Has anyone seen the movie *Hotel Rwanda*? How does it point to the existence of God?

I first saw the movie Hotel Rwanda with my daughter and a group of her friends. In Rwanda, in the space of less than a year, a million people were destroyed, many of them butchered with machetes, for belonging to the wrong tribe. After the movie we went out and talked for a long time, trying to absorb what we had seen. A year or so later I got to meet in real life the central man the film was about, and his dignity and courage are convicting.

Of course, in one sense the problem of evil poses one of the greatest difficulties — for me the greatest — to believing in God. Why he does not stop it is something I don't fully understand.

However, this is another angle. Of all forms of suffering, the worst is that which involves human wickedness. Nazi Germany, Cambodia, and Rwanda are some of our deepest horror stories. But it's hard to see how there could be such a thing as wickedness if naturalism is true.

The category of wickedness makes sense only if people were created and intended to behave a certain way. An accidental universe may have pleasure and pain, but there would be no moral distinction between them, since wickedness can exist only in a moral universe. The reality of evil — not just pain, but evil — is a reason to believe. But it's not the greatest reason. — John Ortberg, *Know Doubt: Embracing Uncertainty in Your Faith* (Grand Rapids, MI: Zondervan, 2014).

20. I ask again: what is the most compelling argument for the Christian faith for you personally?

A guy by the name of Bill Moore, who grew up in poverty, got drunk one time and shot a man for five thousand dollars. He ended up on death row. Lee Strobel met Bill and writes about him in his book The Case for Faith.

A couple of guys went into prison (because God prompts people to go into prisons) and told him, "Bill, there is a man, Jesus, who loves you, and he gave his life on a cross. He died for you. He went to death row for you." Nobody had ever told Bill about Jesus before. He'd been sitting on death row for years. He turned his life over to Jesus, and it changed him so much — changed the darkness and bitterness and hatred inside him so much — that other people began to be drawn to him. People started meeting Jesus through this guy on death row. He became known as "The Peacemaker." His cell block was the safest place in the penitentiary because so many people were coming to Christ through Bill Moore.

Churches found out about this, and when people needed counseling, no kidding, churches started sending people to the penitentiary to get counseling from Bill Moore. Can you imagine calling a church to ask for a referral and hearing, "I want you to go over to death row. There's an inmate there. . . ." What does that? Jesus does that.

Bill Moore was changed so much that he won the love of the family of the man he killed. It changed him so much over the sixteen-year period that all kinds of people wrote letters for him. Eventually, the authorities not only canceled his death sentence; they not only commuted his sentence, which was unprecedented; but they paroled him. Bill Moore now serves as head of congregation in a couple of housing projects in a desperately poor area. When Strobel met with him, he asked, "Bill, what in the world turned your life around? Was it a new medication? Was it some kind of rehab program? Was it a new approach to counseling?"

Bill said, "No, Lee, it wasn't any of that stuff. It was Jesus Christ."

Atheism really has nothing to say to a guy on death row. Because when you're living on death row (and we're all living on death row), there's really only one thing you want to know. — John Ortberg, *Know Doubt: Embracing Uncertainty in Your Faith* (Grand Rapids, MI: Zondervan, 2014).

21. How can we pray for each other this week?

Made in the USA
Coppell, TX
30 September 2021